THE SECRET DANITES KANSAS' FIRST JAYHAWKERS

TODD MILDFELT

Todd Mildfelt Publishing, Richmond, Kansas

Cover photo of Charles Leonhardt courtesy of
Kansas State Historical Society, Topeka.

Cover design by Doug Archer Illustrations, Garnett, Kansas.

The Secret Danites Kansas' First Jayhawkers

© 2003 by Todd Mildfelt

ISBN 0-9743597-0-X

Library of Congress Control Number: 2003095300

All rights reserved. No part of this book may be
reproduced or utilized in any form or by any means,
electronic or mechanical, including photocopying,
recording, or by any information storage and retrieval
system, except by a reviewer who may quote brief
passages in a review to be printed in a magazine
or newspaper, without permission in writing from
the publisher. For information, please contact
Todd Mildfelt Publishing, Richmond, Kansas 66080.

First Edition
Printed in the United States of America
by Central Plains Book Manufacturing, Winfield, Kansas

Edited by Scan Communications Group, Inc., Dubuque, Iowa

THE SECRET DANITES

KANSAS' FIRST

JAYHAWKERS

By

TODD MILDFELT

Dedicated

to all, who fearlessly spoke, wrote or

fought against human Slavery, regardless

of losing their fame, ease, wealth, or Life,

for doing so.

—C. W. Leonhardt
Louisville, Kansas, 1876

(Original dedication by Charles Leonhardt for
the book he worked on called Stray Leaves)

Introduction

Slavery issues began to politically divide the United States as early as the Constitutional Convention in 1787, but compromises were reached for the next 60 years that kept the nation intact. Most of the trouble that began in the mid-1800s stemmed from the large new territories the U.S. had gained and the question arose of how and where slavery would be extended.

In 1854, Congress passed the Kansas-Nebraska Act that created two new territories in the west and opened it for settlement. The act did away with the old Missouri Compromise dividing line and established popular sovereignty—a new method upon which the actual settlers of a territory, instead of Congress, would decide whether the territory would be free or slave. Not only was a large experiment created, one where the settlers would have the power to decide the slavery question for themselves, but also an experiment that would plunge the United States into a whole new, angry contest over the slavery question.

As settlement opened in Kansas in 1854, settlers began to trickle in, and by 1855 communities had been established, most having a distinct slave or free state preference. Violence between the two groups broke out, elections were held that witnessed widespread fraud, and each side elected legislatures to represent its claim as the legitimate, representative body of Kansas.

Into this wild, political cauldron came a man named Charles F. W. Leonhardt. An emigrant from Prussian Poland, he had lived in Plymouth, Massachusetts, for three years before heading to Kansas with a New England Emigrant Aid Society group during the middle of the tumultuous Bleeding Kansas era. Within a matter of months, Leonhardt had made his Free State position clear, been elected to attend the Territorial Legislature in June, 1857, and not only met James H. Lane but was personally inducted by him into a secret organization called the Danites. This secret organization was formed to protect Free State settlers and do everything it could to make Kansas free of its pro-slavery government.

Leonhardt found himself an actor in the unfolding drama of the early throes of civil war and for over two years participated with some of the most famous names of this time, including John Brown,

General James H. Lane, James Montgomery, and the Reverend John Stewart. All of these men had an effect on him, including James Lane, who often told him there was much the public didn't know about the "unwritten history" of Kansas. This was especially true about matters in southeast Kansas where Leonhardt wrote that some of the Danites became the first Jayhawkers.[1] In the 1870s, Charles began writing down what he knew about this "unwritten history" and according to several newspaper accounts had a manuscript ready to be published into a book called "Stray Leaves—the Unwritten History of Kansas."[2] Leonhardt died in 1884 without ever seeing his work published. His wife, Esther, continued unsuccessfully to have the manuscript published until her death in 1892.

At some point, Leonhardt's original manuscript disappeared and was perhaps lost to history forever. This book is my attempt to re-tell a part of that lost story.

Leonhardt's original notes, drafts, and manuscripts, written in quill pen and pencil, have been on deposit at the Kansas State Historical Society in Topeka, Kansas, for over 50 years. These writings are very difficult to decipher, and although known to scholars and some authors, they had been only partially transcribed. I began that task in the summer of 2001 and discovered that Leonhardt had written more about this secret Danite group than any other person. As such, they not only contain valuable insight into Leonhardt's "unwritten history" of Kansas but also help explain a part of some forgotten history of Kansas.

In some of the quotes from the transcriptions of Leonhardt's writings a blank (_____) indicates places where the original words are unreadable.

Todd Mildfelt
Richmond, Kansas
July, 2002

James H. Lane: Served as colonel of an Indiana regiment during the Mexican War, elected lieutenant governor of Indiana in 1849 and to the U.S. House of Representatives in 1852. Moved to Kansas in 1855 with aspirations of becoming a U.S. senator after Kansas entered the union. Chosen general of Kansas militia and President, Topeka Free State Convention. Led a volunteer group of fighters into the state in 1856. Shot and killed Gaius Jenkins over claim dispute, June, 1858, later acquitted. Served as commander of Kansas regiment during the Civil War, elected U.S. senator from Kansas in 1861, committed suicide in 1866.

Reverend John E. Stewart: Born in England, emigrated to the United States. Became a Methodist minister, conducted an early survey in southeast Kansas during the winter of 1856–1857. Listed as the sheriff of the Squatter's Court in Bourbon County. Fought alongside James Montgomery in southeast Kansas in 1857–1858, including "jayhawking" in 1858. Active in Underground Railroad between Kansas and Iowa and later spied for the Union Army during the Civil War.

Charley Lenhart: Free-state man arrived in Kansas in 1855, worked as typesetter for the *Herald of Freedom,* became free state guerilla leader after raid on Lawrence in 1856. Became involved with John Brown and, according to accounts, attempted a rescue of John Brown before his execution and attempted to rescue John Cook. Joined Union Army, became a lieutenant, died in Arkansas in 1863.

John Brown: Notorious free-state leader during Bleeding Kansas. Followed his sons to Kansas in 1855, helped defend Lawrence and Osawatomie. Organized his own free state guerilla group, involved in Pottowatomie Massacre May, 1856. Won first battle between free state and pro-slavery forces at the Battle of Black Jack, June 2, 1856. Involved in Underground Railroad activity and later led a failed raid against the federal arsenal at Harper's Ferry, Virginia, where he planned to capture guns and arm slaves in a large slave revolt but was captured. Hung in December, 1859, his death helped serve notice to the nation that compromises on slavery were a thing of the past.

James Montgomery: Free-state settler in Linn County, Kansas. Assumed leadership position in guerilla fighting in southeast Kansas in 1857. Leader of over 200 men for a short while, was first to organize a guerilla group that became known as Jayhawkers. Went east to participate in an aborted rescue attempt of some of John Brown's men. Later, commanded a Kansas regiment during the Civil War. Returned to Linn County after the war, died in 1872.

Acknowledgments

I would like to thank the many people who assisted me in the writing of this book. This would include the staff at the Kansas State Historical Society in Topeka, Lyon County Historical Society, Swan River Museum, Linn County Historical Society, Franklin County Historical Archives, Ottawa Public Library, Osawatomie Public Library, Iola Public Library, and the Plymouth Public Library, Plymouth, Massachusetts.

I would like to acknowledge the special assistance of Herman Weiland, great grandson of Charles Leonhardt and the late Dorothy Branson, great granddaughter of Leonhardt. Mr. Weiland was my sounding board for ideas and theories in the early stages of my research and provided great help in keeping me on my path. Others who provided valuable advice and assistance include Judy Sweets, Willa Wilson, Herman Hunt, Jo Ann Henning, Ola May Earnest, Deb Barker, Tim Rues, Bob Knecht, and Teresa Coble.

As a final note of appreciation, I would like to acknowledge the valuable help by the late Myrtle Ziergiebel, who lived in Kingston, Massachusetts. Her genealogical research on Leonhardt in the 1980s uncovered important information and benefited me greatly.

KANSAS TERRITORY
1857-1858

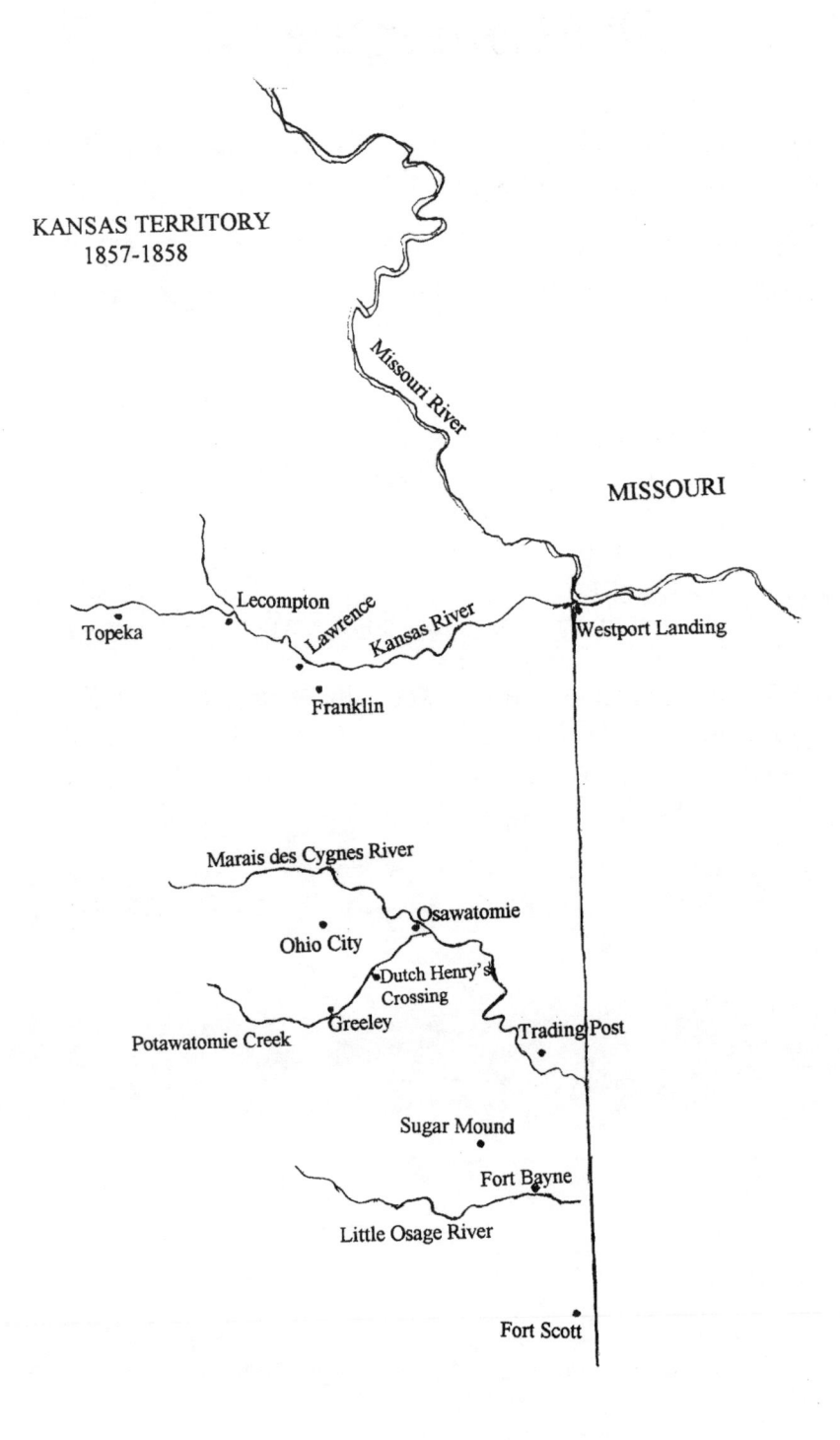

Missouri River

MISSOURI

Topeka
Lecompton
Lawrence
Kansas River
Westport Landing
Franklin

Marais des Cygnes River
Osawatomie
Ohio City
Dutch Henry's Crossing
Potawatomie Creek
Greeley
Trading Post

Sugar Mound
Fort Bayne
Little Osage River

Fort Scott

Contents

    Introduction . . . . *v*
1 Trouble around Lawrence. *1*
2 The Danites *8*
3 Charles Leonhardt *13*
4 Into the Epicenter. *19*
5 The Danites in Action *32*
6 James Lane and His Danites *50*
7 John Brown and the Danites *69*
8 John Brown and Harper's Ferry *77*
9 Danites Reunited *83*
10 Charles Leonhardt/Charles Lenhart *88*
11 Conclusion *99*
    Epilogue *107*
    Appendix *109*
    Notes *110*
    Bibliography *122*
    Index *127*

> Be it enacted by that noble hand
> Of Border Ruffians bowie knife in hand
> Should a sneaking Yankee from the East
> Come here and dare to meddle in the least
> With our Niggers be they dark as night
> Or those in whom we have mixed a little white
> Any man of Southern blood and vote
> Shall cut his cursed AntiSlavery throat
>
> signed G. I. N. _____
> Speaker of the first Ks territorial Legislature

signed
O.L.D. Bourbon
President Ks first Legislature

(Author's note: John Stringfellow was the first Speaker of the Territorial Legislature and Thomas Johnson the first Senate President. Gin and Bourbon must be Leonhardt's nicknames.)

1

Trouble around Lawrence

On the afternoon of November 21, 1855, a free-state settler named Charles Dow, who shared a cabin with a man named Jacob Branson at a site about 15 miles south of the year-old town of Lawrence, was accosted by a neighbor, Frank Coleman. It was not the first time the two men had angry words but for Dow it would be the last. On this day, Coleman took a gun and shot Dow, killing him. And while the altercation stemmed mostly from an argument over a land claim and the cutting of timber,[1] the fact remained that a pro-slavery man had shot and killed a free-state man, and this so close to Lawrence, the free-state bastion started by settlers of the New England Emigrant Aid Society and ably led by Charles Robinson, who a few years earlier had gained experience in the rough and tumble California land riots around Sacramento during which he had shot a man and was seriously wounded himself.[2]

The pro-slavery settlers had already gained an early advantage by winning the election on March 30, 1855, and had established a territorial government favoring slavery. Although they had a majority of settlers at the time, the pro-slavery forces participated in the widespread fraud of having Missourians cross into Kansas and vote illegally in addition to intimidating free-state voters and preventing many of them from voting. In spite of the fact that the election loss was seen as a setback, some of the free-state leaders hoped as Charles Robinson did that if they could "persist and never, in any instance, be cowed into silence or subserviency to their dictation,"[3] then they "might hope to hang on and pray for a better day."[4]

Up until the killing of Dow, in this potentially explosive situation that Kansas found itself, the struggle between pro-slavery and free-state settlers had largely been one of harassing words, threats, intimidations, and tar and feathers. To be sure, there had been an incident in Leavenworth on April 30, 1855, where a free-state man named Cole McCrea shot and killed a pro-slavery man named Malcolm Clarke. McCrea was put in jail and escaped and his friend, who refused to leave town, was eventually tarred and feathered, but no further retribution was exacted.[5] But if one wants to find an early turning point in the period of Bleeding Kansas one need look no further than the shooting of Charles Dow. It was this shooting that lit the fuse that would burn through 1855 and finally explode in the spring of 1856 into a microcosm of civil war between pro-slavery and free-state forces. More than the shooting alone, the incident set in motion a chain of events that continued to escalate. Five days later, while men in the surrounding area met and discussed what they should do about it, a posse of pro-slavery men led by the questionable sheriff of Douglas County, Samuel Jones, burst into Branson's house and took him prisoner. The free-state men felt that as "Branson was the principal witness against Coleman in the Dow murder case . . . an attempt was being made to put the old man out of the way in order to clear Coleman.[6] The authority of the sheriff was in question because he had been appointed by the territorial legislature that free-staters didn't recognize due to the fraudulent nature of the election of March 30, 1855, and the fact they didn't feel Jones was a legal resident of Kansas.

On the evening of the arrest of Branson, a rescue party was hurriedly put together and set about trying to locate the whereabouts of the posse. This party, led by Sam Wood and James Abbott, had spent hours trying to discover some trace of where the posse had gone, when long after dark, all of a sudden the posse rode over a hill, riding along the trail that would take them right by Abbott's cabin. As the free-state men spread across the road, the posse halted and one of their men asked, "What's up?" When the free-state men said they wanted Branson, the pro-slavery men answered he would be shot if he moved. With guns cocked on both sides, the situation was only a hair's breadth from two dozen men shooting it out on the star-lit trail.[7] And then Branson said, "I will come if they do shoot" and pushed the mule he was riding forward while guns were trained on his back.[8] It was possibly only this courageous act by Branson that averted serious bloodshed that night. Sheriff Jones pled his case to the free-state men for almost an hour, saying he had a warrant for this prisoner and had to take him in but in the end, he left empty-handed.[9]

The taking away of Branson from the posse was exactly what the pro-slavery forces had been waiting for, a flagrant act by the free-state forces usurping the authority of the bogus government and giving pro-slavers the opportunity, under the cover of legality, to crush the free-state power base in Lawrence.

Calls went out all over Missouri to retaliate, and true to its script a large army of over 2,000 men eventually assembled and in effect laid siege to Lawrence in what is known as the Wakarusa War. Although the conflict was called a war, the two sides faced each other with no real attack being made. Lawrence was turned into an armed camp, with breastworks and redoubts manned by men, many of whom were armed with Sharp's rifles. Charles Robinson continued his leadership role and had been chosen as a de facto general of the militia, having been joined by James H. Lane, veteran commander of an Indiana regiment from the Mexican War, who had been in Lawrence since April 20, 1855, and had accepted a leadership role.[10]

Armed patrols scouted the countryside while most of the men stayed in their camps. On December 6, two men from a nearby pro-slavery patrol caught up with free-staters Thomas Barber, his brother Robert and brother-in-law, Thomas Pierson. When told they would have to go with the pro-slavers as prisoners Tom replied, "We won't do it." One of the two ruffians, named George Clarke, drew his pistol and fired, hitting Tom. Robert got off a few shots and the parties broke apart. Although they galloped away, Tom Barber made it only a few hundred yards before he fell out of the saddle and was dead.[11]

Later that evening the territorial governor, Wilson Shannon, arrived in Lawrence to see what could be done to ease the tension and end the stand-off. After a meeting with the leaders of both sides it was agreed the free-staters could keep their weapons but would obey territorial laws in the future. In effect many Missourians felt they had been sold out and were still in favor of making an attack and probably would have if not for a major winter storm that struck and finally drove the Missourians home.[12]

Although the Wakarusa War had ended, no one thought the troubles were over. For some of the free-state men around Lawrence, however, they now had seen enough to convince them something else needed to be done and that something was to organize a secret society, "the purposes of which were to retaliate against the ruffians for the crimes they were committing."[13] James Lane, already given quasi-sanction as a military leader for the free-state militia, was also given the chance to be one of the leaders of this new secret society. For Lane, who had come to Kansas looking for the opportunity to assume a leadership role in shaping territorial Kansas, including hopes for the U.S. Senate, this was a chance not to be wasted.

According to D. W. Wilder in his *Annals of Kansas*, the funeral of Tom Barber took place on December 16, 1855, and on the 22nd of December a "secret society of Free-State men formed this year at Lawrence, [and] are variously called "Defenders," "Regulators," and "Danites."[14]

Secret groups were certainly nothing new to the United States in the mid-1850s and as there were already secret societies both for and against slavery, it was natural they found their way into Kansas, with both sides pushing settlers to go and stake a claim there. On the pro-slavery side there were the Blue Lodges, Social Bands, and Dark Lantern Societies. Spring (1885) related that, for the election in 1854, "Western Missouri was armed and equipped to assail abolitionists in the territory. For this purpose Blue Lodges—a species of semi-secret, counter–Massachusetts societies designed to operate at Kansas elections—had been extensively organized. . . . The 29th of November at all events would afford opportunity for a little experimenting to see what seeds of promise lay in the Blue Lodges"[15] and he credits these organizations for the large number, 1,729, of illegal votes by Missourians.[16]

Phillips (1856) and Gihon (1857) both related the findings of a congressional investigation into secret slavery societies and found that the Missouri secret groups were:

> known by different names, such as "Social Band," "Friends Society," "Blue Lodge," "The Sons of the South." Its members were bound together by secret oaths, and they had passwords, signs, and grips, by which they were known to each other. Penalties were imposed for violating the rules and secrets of the order. Written minutes were kept of the proceedings of the lodges, and the different lodges were connected together by an effective organization. It embraced great numbers of the citizens of Missouri, and was extended into other slave states and into the territory. Its avowed purpose was not only to extend slavery into Kansas, but also into other territory of the United States, and to form a union of all the friends of that institution. Its plan of operating was to organize and send men to vote at the elections in the territory. . . . It also proposed to induce pro-slavery men to emigrate into the territory, to aid and sustain them while there, and to elect none

to office but those friendly to their views. . . . In its lodges in Missouri the affairs of Kansas were discussed, the force necessary to control the election was divided into bands, and leaders selected, means were collected, and signs and badges were agreed upon.[17]

On the free-state side was a group called the Wide-Awakes, a group that one participant described as "a secret antislavery order, [it] had been organized and spread to Kansas, and absorbed about every free-state man in the territory."[18] In Leonhardt's account of an Underground Railroad trip he accompanied to Iowa in 1860 he related that, in Des Moines, "Here in the Capitol of Iowa we beheld in 'Washburn' the first Captain of the regular 'Wide-Awakes,'"[19] so some kind of connection with the Danites seems apparent.

Although the existence of some of these secret groups is frequently mentioned by writers of the period, very little is actually known about their organization and activities, but being secret that would stand to reason. Leonhardt wrote about the Danites that "those of my fellow Kansans who needed this mystical cloak and binding secrecy of the order for the purpose of cementing them to more energetic Action, against the great foe, did but right to join the Order. Among all the Nations the American people find the greatest delight in all sorts of secret organization."[20]

According to James Legate, quoted in Richard Hinton's book *John Brown and His Men*, the:

> forming [of] the Danites [in Lawrence] . . . had its birth because of the murder of Dow, Barber, and the robbing and house-burning that were frequent in those days. . . . James H. Lane was a member and a leader. John Speer, Charles Robinson, Captain Shore, and many others whose names I cannot recall, were members. Charles Robinson, however soon failed to attend, becoming more earnest in his Boston theory of non-resistance. The society had not much more than a year's duration, because Lane was continuously calling meetings, and would invariably have a long paper of "whereas" Bill Smith, a "pro-slavery hell hound" had been guilty of stealing free-state men's horses, or burning someone's house, or some crime of less grade, and then, "Therefore Resolved" that Bill Smith shall be brought before this body of men, his case investigated and adjudicated, and the decree shall be executed by one or men appointed by the commander of this council, or of some sub-council. Lane's "Whereas" killed the society.[21]

Leonhardt supports part of Legate's statement, saying, "if there were no Ruffians handy to be kicked, we would do the next to it, draw up resolution after resolution Always profaning them, to be parliamentary in our Doings: Whereas, Missourians are again threatning [sic] our borders, therefore resolved: We are ready for you! After this huge & patriotic work was at last accomplished we would go home _____ triumphantly."[22]

Legate's comments appear to be mostly accurate. Robinson was a short-lived member, and admitted it himself in his own book. However, what Legate failed to learn was that the Danites did not end in a little more than a year's time but broke away from the Lawrence headquarters group, first under Lane, and then a more radical group broke away from Lane himself!

After the Wakarusa War, events continued that were related to it. Sheriff Jones came to Lawrence in April, 1856, to serve writs on some of those involved in the Branson rescue and was shot while standing in Lt. James McIntosh's tent.[23] Although seriously wounded and reported as dead, Jones survived, but pro-slavery forces in Missouri saw in this another opportunity to besiege Lawrence and this time their forces were more effective in exacting revenge. A month after Jones was shot, Lawrence was raided. The *Kansas Free State* and the *Herald of Freedom* newspaper offices were wrecked, and the Free-State Hotel and other buildings were destroyed. Three days later, with the tide of battle swaying to the pro-slavery side, John Brown and a few men killed five pro-slavery settlers along the Pottawatomie Creek at Dutch Henry's Crossing, now Lane, Kansas. This lightning bolt, known as the Pottawatomie Massacre, came at the exact time the pro-slavery men seemed to have re-taken the advantage, stung pro-slavery forces, and set the whole countryside on its ear. Small groups of pro-slavery forces swept into Kansas again; Brown and 15 men met one of these groups and defeated it in the first actual battle between opposing forces in Kansas at the Battle of Black Jack near Baldwin. Federal troops had been called out and they met up with Brown and forced him to release his prisoners.

In July, federal troops disbanded the free-state legislature meeting at Topeka, Charles Robinson and other leaders were taken prisoner by pro-slave forces, and free-state forces faced a new low. It was at this time, when almost all hope seemed lost, that James Lane returned to Kansas ahead of a loose collection of volunteers who were coming to help make Kansas a free state. The Free-State forces raided the pro-slavery town of Franklin a few miles east of Lawrence and captured a cannon, then used it to defeat pro-slavery forces at Saunders and Fort Titus. A few months later, a large contingent of pro-slavery forces arrived outside of Osawatomie, killed one of John Brown's sons, then defeated a small force of defenders led by Brown and burned almost every building in the town. Although by the fall of 1856, the pro-slavery forces could mount a strong attacking force, it was becoming clearer that free-state forces were slowly gaining the advantage of numbers inside Kansas, and a larger wave of free-state settlers would be coming in the spring of 1857.

2

The Danites

Returning to December, 1855, and the end of the Wakarusa War, we pick up again the formation of the Danites. An interesting choice of names, the word *Danite*, or literally son of Dan, is first found in the Bible mentioned in the book of Judges, chapter 13, verse 2. As the children of Israel had sinned the Lord delivered them into the hand of the Philistines 40 years. "And there was a certain man of Zorah, of the family of the Danites, whose name *was* Manoah; and his wife *was* barren, and bare not." Manoah's wife did bare him a son after a visit from an angel and the son's name was Sampson.[1] In chapter 18, Danite is mentioned again. "In those days, there was no king in Israel: and in those days the tribe of the Danites sought them an inheritance to dwell in. . . . And the children of Dan sent of their family five men from their coasts, men of valor . . . to spy out the land." These men determined that the land called Laish was good and worth taking and told their brethren they will fight for this land. "And there went from thence of the family of the Danites, out of Zorah and out of Eshtaol, 600 men appointed with weapons of war." These 600 men and the five went to Laish to Micah's house and took his priests and graven images; "they smote them with the edge of the sword, and burnt the city with fire." They built their own city, called Dan, and the priests of Micah became their priests.[2]

From these passages one can deduce the meaning of a Danite to be a member of the tribe of Dan but more specifically one that is good with weapons and sent on a mission to take new lands. Certainly the relationship to what was happening in Kansas was not lost on the men of Lawrence.

I have found no mention of the word *Danite* between its biblical usage and the 1800s when it first appeared with reference to a secret group associated with the Mormons in 1838. The Mormons, after organizing their church in New York, moved into Missouri and were harassed and persecuted in Jackson County and later Clay and Caldwell Counties. A small group of Mormons was organized from members that had become more radical in how they wanted to deal with the persecution and began trying to fight back. This Mormon group, called Daughters of Zion, Destroying Angels, and finally Danites, tried to operate as a secret group charged with protecting the Mormons from the Gentiles. Led by Jared Carter and Sampson Avard, this group had little success in preventing attacks on the Mormons in Missouri. Later, after the Mormons had moved to Utah, a Danite group was again active as trouble broke out between the Mormons and the federal government and parties of settlers moving west.[3]

Leonhardt was aware of the Mormon Danites and later wrote "the Secret Order of the Kansas Danites must have strayed from the pacific slope. The Danites of Utah were known as the destroying Angels in their attempt to resist the march of the gentiles among them. They fought to perpetuate a most peculiar institution we here in Kansas to utter [sic] annihilate a very heinous one."[4]

The Danite group organized in Lawrence in 1855 initially was formed as a protection group and was not inclined to offensive behavior. Its lack of action and Lane's preoccupation with minutia are given as reasons for its end.[5] This Danite group that formed in Lawrence met in the Masonic Hall and had a grand master, priests and other levels of degrees, a secret grip and signs,[6] its own secret cipher,[7] and a secret oath.

Frank Blackmar, in his *Kansas A Cyclopedia of State History*, written in 1912, noted this about the Danites: "In the state archives of the Kansas Historical Society the writer found several cipher dispatches sent by one 'encampment' to another, . . . officers went by number instead of by name."[8] This information agrees with what Wendall Stephenson wrote about the Danites in 1928 in his *Publication of the Kansas State Historical Society*. In a footnote about the Danites Stephenson noted, "Some Danite lodge correspondence, a part of it written in cipher, is preserved in the Kansas Historical Society Archives, the letters bear the dates [January 26, 1858] March 3, 27, April 19, May 1, 14, 27."[9] These seven letters in the State Historical Society Archives show a high level of organization that connected the different Danite lodges together.[10] (More on these letters appears in chapter 6.)

A copy of the Danite secret oath, one similar to the secret oath taken by the Freemasons,[11] was published in the *Leavenworth Herald* on July 24, 1858, and is as follows:

> I _____ _____, in the most solemn manner, here, in the presence of Heaven and these witnesses, bind myself that I will never reveal, nor cause to be revealed, either by word, look, sign, by writing, printing, engraving, painting, or in any manner whatsoever, anything pertaining to this institution, save to persons duly qualified to receive them. I will never reveal the nature of the organization, the place of meeting, the fact that any person is a member of the same, or even the existence of the organization, except to persons legally qualified to receive the same. Should I at any time withdraw, or be suspended or expelled from this organization, I will keep this obligation to the end of my life. If any books, papers, or monies belonging to this organization be entrusted to my keeping, I will faithfully and completely deliver up the same to my successor in office, or any one legally authorized to receive them. I will never knowingly propose a person for membership in this order who is not in favor of making KANSAS A FREE STATE, and whom I feel satisfied will exert his entire influence to bring about this result. I will support, maintain, and abide by any movement made by this organization to secure this great end. I will unflinchingly vote for and support the candidates nominated by this organization in preference to any and all others. To all this obligation I do most solemnly promise and affirm, binding myself under the penalty of being expelled from this organization, of having my name published to the several territorial encampments as a perjurer before Heaven and a traitor to my country of passing through life scorned and reviled by man, frowned on by devils, forsaken by angels, and abandoned by God.[12]

Obviously the fact that a pro-slavery newspaper such as the *Leavenworth Herald* published this oath indicates the paper was seeking to exploit the publicity as propaganda showing just how far the free-state forces had gone in their attempt to make Kansas free, as well as offering proof that a Danite organization did exist, which was debatable at the time.

Unfortunately the oath stands alone in this issue. There is no other commentary about the oath, how the paper obtained a copy of it, or anything else which might further shed light on the Danites. One might suppose that James Redpath, a former Danite who had in May, 1858, implicated Lane in a murder plot against Governor Denver, was also the one who leaked the secret oath to the *Leavenworth Herald* in July, 1858. More on this plot will be discussed in chapter 6.

Using Andreas' *History of Kansas*, one finds "in 1855 an association was formed by certain disaffected parties in Doniphan for the purpose of opposing obnoxious laws. This body was known as the Danites; Patrick Laughlin, a tinsmith of the town, joined this Society, but on becoming aware of its full purpose became disgusted and openly proclaimed all of its secrets," and then, after describing how the Danites tried to wreak vengeance on the traitor, including an attempt to kill Laughlin, the account concludes by saying, "This was the end of the Danites."[13]

Holloway (1868) gave additional information on this incident and the Danites when he noted that after the:

> "continued threatening and armed demonstrations of the Missourians ... accordingly a secret order of a military character was introduced, (the Kansas Legion,) similar to the Blue Lodges of Missouri, with this exception—its object was solely defensive, while that of the latter was offensive. Its design was to labor by all lawful means to make Kansas a free State, and to protect the ballot-box from invasion. There was nothing wrong in the Society itself, nor in its object, or means employed to attain that object. It never extended far over the Territory. There were, however, several 'encampments' at different places. It was secret in its character, and the members took an obligation in accordance with the nature and design of the society. It was found to be too cumbrous and unwieldy, and soon fell into disuse...."[14]

Continuing on, Holloway stated "This is the society which Pat Loughland [Laughlin] claimed to expose,"[15] indicating that the Kansas Legion and the Danites were one in the same.

Blackmar (1912) came to the conclusion that these early historians who wrote about the Danites were "in error ... [in their belief] that the society did not last long, and that it was of a defensive character only."[16] Speaking of the secret dispatches, Blackmar wrote, "None of them throws any light on the subject that tends to show when the Danites were organized or when they disbanded. Nor do any of the documents bear out Holloway's suggestion that the society was organized purely for defense."[17]

By using Leonhardt's manuscripts, I have now been able to answer these questions and more. Leonhardt's writings help fill in many of the gaps, and it now seems certain that the Danite group that formed in

December, 1855, was done so as a self-protection group for free-state men in and around Lawrence, and then other groups soon sprang up. These groups languished through 1856 and most of 1857 with no real action or accomplishments other than the organization itself. Writing about the Lawrence group, Leonhardt said:

> Among the grand master or other High priests of the Kansas Danites I have utterly failed to behold the very first healthy looking fruit from that wonderful tree, they pretended of having planted, nourished and cared for, they might have coaxed here and there a sound looking bud to appear, but ripe fruit under their fostering care alone, is NEVER brought forth. They had to all appearances exhausted their last energies after successfully establishing the Head center at Lawrence. These wise men had entirely forgotten that Liberty is a very peculiar and tender plant, that sometimes must be watered with blood. If they actually knew this to be a fact they very shrewdly left this particular dangerous branch of its culture for the common workers of the Order to accomplish. This class of men, was indeed for the welfare of the cause at Heart, what rootlets and leaves are to the giant Oak, insignificant in themselves, but without them, life soon ceases. Their many trials and untold sacrifices will here become known to the outside unfeeling world. Those who were called away from us to wear the crown of the martyr or become kripple [sic] for Life, have their families not remembered.[18]

At some point in 1857, Lane decided to take control of the group and use it for his own purposes. A smaller group of Danites then broke away from Lane to pursue their own objectives in southeast Kansas, while at the same time Lane's plans for assassination and rebellion were attempted and fell apart. Lane temporarily lost most of his influence and power after he shot and killed Gaius Jenkins in a personal dispute. He was indicted in June, 1858, and later acquitted. Leonhardt bears this out, noting, "with Lane's homicide in June, the 3, killing Gaius Jenkins, we he went under a heavy Cloud and left us actual [sic] without a military Leader even in name. And that was well in the end, for all concerned."[19] Much of the need for the Danites fell apart at this time with peace arriving in southeast Kansas. When violence again flared in the region in the fall of 1858, some of the remaining Danites again took the field, along with a few others, and became known then as "Jayhawkers." Even after peace finally arrived in February, 1859, the Danites still were not finished. Remnants of the Danites/Jayhawkers continued their ties and activities by becoming more active in the Underground Railroad.

3

Charles Leonhardt

Since very little is known about the Kansas Danites and the basis of this book is the writings of Charles Leonhardt, it would do well for readers to know more about the man. Born on May 13, 1827, in Grottkau, Prussia, according to newspaper accounts of his life, Leonhardt had a classsical education[1] but then joined the Prussian army. Leonhardt was in and out of active duty between 1847 and 1852,[2] but according to his own story he joined the Hungarian Revolution in 1848, fighting the yoke of oppression against the Austrians.[3]

The Hungarian Revolt, under the leadership of Louis Kossuth, had initial success until the Austrians allowed Russia to help them and the Russian army put down the revolt in 1849 and kept the Austrian monarchy in power. According to family history, Charles had an extraordinary career in this revolt and even fled the country with Kossuth. None of this had been substantiated and the stories of some of Charles' deeds seem doubtful. There is an inconsistency between his obituary saying he arrived in the United States in 1849 and his citizenship application, which says he arrived May 19, 1854. He was granted a passport valid for one year beginning December 4, 1849,[4] so it is possible he left the country in 1849 and returned to Germany sometime in 1850 and resumed his military service. The 1854 date on his arrival in the U.S. would suggest that he was not in any hurry to leave his country, but Leonhardt later wrote that the revolution caused him to seek a home in America.[5] Further, the dates on his naturalization certificate suggest that Leonhardt was able to circumvent the statute that said the naturalization process was five years. If the dates on his papers are correct he was naturalized after three years.

Although I have been unable to verify Charles' participation in the Hungarian Revolution, he claimed in his later writings that the conflict in Kansas was similar to the one he participated in during his homeland struggles and reflected:

I had received the bloody baptism of fire on some of the European battle fields in the eventful years of 1846 to 1849 inclusive when Germany, Poland and Hungary attempted to throw off the galling yoke of the tyrants. Great as these events have been . . . I am compelled to place them in background, when compared with the mighty uproar and toils of the great anti-slavery tumult here, in the home of my adoption. . . . It need not surprise any one that he who unsheathed his sword on the banks of the Danube should also be found eager and anxious to assist in boldly kicking the images of human slavery out of the lands of liberty. . . . In every borderrufian [sic] I recognized the hired tool of crowned heads, though he badly lacked their glittering battle array. . . .[6]

Certainly if, as he claimed, Leonhardt did participate in the Hungarian struggle, this experience stood him in good stead for moving to New England in the 1850s and adopting wholeheartedly the views of abolitionism that were running strong. Landing first in New York, he wandered to Maine and learned to speak English in the home of one who took him in.[7] Leonhardt then moved south as he "wanted to see first hand where the Pilgrims landed."[8] While living in Plymouth, Massachusetts, in 1854, Charles applied for U.S. citizenship.[9] Midway through his citizenship period, the Kansas Territory opened for settlement and the contest to make it free or slave became a dominant issue in New England. As the struggle turned violent and stories raced from the virgin plains, Charles felt his "pulses pounding" for free Kansas. He wrote a poem in German that was translated and included in the Plymouth *Old Colony Memorial*, June 28, 1856, and possibly read at a Kansas recruitment meeting:

A Voice for Kansas

Hark: I hear the trumpets sounding:
Hark: 'tis Freedom's dying call:
And I feel my pulses pounding
As my burning tear-drops fall
    Dare I surely,
    Or securely,
Speak my protest to this time:
Where the children of one mother,
North and South oppose each other,
Each in Freedom's name sublime.

Ah! they haste with vain endeavor
To that blood-stained western plain,
Where so many fall forever -
Fall alas, returning never,
To their Northern homes again.
    Ah! a yearning,
    Bitter burning,
Kindles up a fire unknown -
North and South will strive together,
One at least will crush the other,
Under Freedom's sacred throne.

What the Future may afford us,
Waiteth trembling every breeze,
If when passed these woes that awed us,
Peace shall bloom within our borders,
With the Future still must rest
    Tears of yearning,
    Life-blood burning,
Still shall flow like summer rain -
Till men, brotherly united
Raise poor Kansas crushed and blighted
To her throne of peace again.[10]

    Speeches were given in Plymouth during the summer of 1856 and the New England Emigrant Aid Society was recruiting men to move to Kansas but Charles had undertaken the enterprise of opening a gymnasium and as yet was not ready to answer the call. One can speculate that Charles was waiting only for his citizenship application to be official before making the move, because when it happened on December 3, 1856, Charles began around this time the process of joining a New England Emigrant Aid Society group, although the exact timing is unclear.[11]

    There is one account, written by friend and fellow Danite Richard Hinton, that claimed Leonhardt came to Kansas in September, 1856,[12] but Hinton must be mistaken on his date. A series of articles and advertisements in the Plymouth newspapers beginning on May 31, 1856, specifically detail the planning, opening, and operation of Charles' gymnasium, known as the "Plymouth Rock." These ads, running until January, 1857, clearly show Leonhardt was operating his gym through the fall of 1856 and his final citizenship papers show he was there in Massachusetts to sign them on December 3, 1856.[13]

Once the new year turned, however, Charles must have been planning the move to Kansas and, for a single man not yet 30 years of age, going to Kansas to help make it a free state may have seemed just what he was looking for.

In an interview in Lawrence, Kansas, in June, 1857, with a correspondent from the Plymouth *Old Colony Memorial* paper, Leonhardt stated he had arrived in Kansas in March and settled about 80 miles south on the very edge of civilization and claimed 160 acres.[14] From these items, it is clear Charles arrived in Lawrence in early March of 1857 and immediately moved to the new settlement of Emporia, where he staked a land claim. There he was instrumental in helping form a free-state military organization which commenced its beginning on June 1, 1857, at the close of the polls.[15] "A committee consisting of Messrs. Anams, Leonhardt, and Larabee, were appointed to draft a constitution, and report at the next meeting. . . ."[16]

Charles was also quickly elected to fill a vacancy as a delegate to the Territorial Legislature and went to Topeka in early June to attend this convention. On June 10, 1857, Leonhardt's credentials were examined and certificates of election certified: "Mess [sic] Arney, Leonhardt, Foster, Harvey, Beach, & Carver being present the oath of office was administered and they entered upon the discharge of the duties of their office."[17] It is interesting to note that in this write-up on the legislative session they misspelled Leonhardt's name* four different ways.[18] The misspelling of his name would be a common occurrence throughout this period of his life.

It is unknown when Leonhardt first met General James Lane. Lane had been active in Lawrence from April, 1855, to early 1856, then left and returned August 11, 1856, ahead of a large volunteer army he recruited to help in the free-state struggle. Lane left on another tour back east to gain support for his actions in Kansas and returned March 3, 1857. This is the same time-frame that Leonhardt arrived in Kansas. Whether or not they were in the same traveling group is unknown.

But if Lane and Leonhardt had not previously met before June, 1857, they surely met at this convention because Lane was chairman

---

*Leonhardt's name appears as Lenhalt, Lenhart, Leonhart and Lionhardt in addition to the correct spelling of Leonhardt. It is only fair to point out, however, that he used the spelling of Lionhardt himself on occasion, as it is spelled that way on his law school graduation bulletin, Ohio Bar certificate and Civil War papers.

and spoke both before and after Leonhardt. On the afternoon of June 9, Leonhardt spoke in favor of Judge Conway's substitute resolution to dissent from the business committee's proposal to "recommend to the Free State Party of Kansas that the election for delegates, in pursuance of the law enacted by the Lecompton bogus Legislature, be disregarded and permitted to pass without any participation therein by the Free State party of Kanzas."[19] Leonhardt's speech that day was carried by the Emporia paper:

> Gentlemen and Fellow Citizens—After listening to these speakers, my spirit has gone back to Europe, and my mind recalls scenes in which I have been an actor on bloody battlefields. I allude to these things not on personal grounds, but because the struggle here [is] a similar one. As a representative from the 6th district, I have a duty to perform. My constituents defined my duties in my capacity of Representation. These duties are in full accordance with my feelings. I see that among the freedom loving men here, there are two parties. One of them says "wait" but the other says "go on." So it was in the Hungarian Revolution. When we could have beaten the Austrians a portion said "wait till we are stronger." We waited until the Russians came and we were overthrown. Here they say wait and see what your Governor will do, he promises us railroads and many other things. I have not much faith in him. His acts are suspicious. Timeo danos et dona ferestes [I fear the Greeks though they come with presents]. When we are ready for railroads we will build them ourselves. We foreign-born citizens heard the wail of Freedom in Kansas—we were bound to listen to that cry. I speak for the adopted citizens when I say we are with you in the fight. We will not shrink. We are Americans by choice and are proud of our chosen land. The people of the 6th District wish to put the carriage in motion, and they ask of others to help them. They wish to organize under the State Government. They do not wish to wait.[20]

Another delegate, T. D. Thatcher, followed Leonhardt, and General Lane followed Thatcher. Although Lane disagreed with Leonhardt on favoring Conway's resolution,[21] he may have been impressed with Leonhardt's passion and substance in not being willing to wait and interpreted in him a readiness for action.

One intriguing irony is the fact that, while serving as lieutenant governor of Indiana in 1851, James Lane met and entertained exiled Hungarian revolutionary leader Louis Kossuth as Kossuth traveled through America on a speaking tour.[22] The same revolutionary leader whom Leonhardt was reported to have served under in Hungary.

Following the legislative session in late July, the 6th district around the Emporia area was changed to the 14th district.[23] Leonhardt was nominated for state senator from this new district[24] and in the August 1, 1857, election received over 200 votes.[25] Leonhardt spent the remaining part of the summer of 1857 on a speaking circuit and told the Massachusetts reporter he had at least 36 speaking engagements scheduled.[26]

Leonhardt's whirlwind summer made big impressions and is evidenced by a letter from Samuel Tappan to Thomas W. Higginson. Higginson was a well-known abolitionist in Boston and a member of the Secret Six, the eastern group that was secretly providing funds to John Brown. Tappan stated, "Lionhardt is a true man, eloquent, enthusiastically alive to the issue here."[27] In September, Rev. Daniel Foster also wrote Higginson and asked for his help in arranging some initial engagements for a lecture tour he and Leonhardt would soon embark on.[28]

Sometime around October 1, Leonhardt accompanied Reverend Foster from Osawatomie to Massachusetts to begin this tour speaking about the state of affairs in Kansas.[29] Leonhardt returned to Kansas in early to mid-December and immediately on his return was made General Lane's adjutant and ordered south to Fort Scott.[30] The date for his return is given as December 18, 1857, in the Emporia paper, but this hardly allows for any time to be appointed Lane's adjutant. If the date is accurate, this would indicate that Lane and Leonhardt had already agreed on the appointment before he went back east. Also, the Emporia paper was in error in that Leonhardt was ordered to Sugar Mound (Mound City), not Fort Scott. Fort Scott was at the time, and had been, a pro-slavery stronghold for all of southeast Kansas and figured in Leonhardt's life for the next 12 months.

4

Into the Epicenter

As more free-state settlers arrived in Kansas during the same time that Leonhardt arrived the situation in Douglas and other northeastern counties improved for the free-state cause, but the fall of 1857 saw the trouble shift to the area around the Little Osage River in southeast Kansas. "What reason does 'Stray Leaves' assign that the troubles in the border counties from 1856 to 1860 are still so terrible misrepresented even by our former friends?"[1] Leonhardt asked this question in 1876 and answered in this way:

> Every one of these many Kansas writers, even those of acknowledged great journalistic form in their most beautiful flowery sentiment and well rounded phrases, have always, from some cause entirely neglected to narrate the true parts of the Outgoing of the Slavepower from Kansas. Of the March into Kansas they wrote and astonished the world with their graphic accounts of the many crimes committed by the slave oligarchic all along the banks of the muddy Missouri or near the oak clad hills and through the green carpeted Dales & valleys of the sleepy, sandy Kaw River till indeed 'bleeding Kansas' became the best advertised Country of Creation. The hordes of Ruffian invaders concentrated for their destruction in Kansas wars in Douglas Co. and every turn in their long and bending trail into Kansas has been noted by these Warrchorrespondances [sic] and correct field notes have been preserved to History. But upon the Outgoing of the slave power from Kansas but meager or very lying reports do exist. How did that horde of Ruffians leave? Did they retrase [sic] their triumphant march with flying banners under martial music as they had come to sack Lawrence? Not much! Did they than [sic] stampede like any other headless mob when scared? They had lost much _____ for that. They skedaddled [sic]! But only the lowest class of these skedaddling stragglers stopped at the border counties or went _____ into Missouri for the purpose of coming back into the border District, in order to satisfy their thirst for more human blood. It was _____ now consolidated remnants of former Ruffian squads who made Lykins, Linn &

Bourbon Counties their fields of operation & whose bloody footprints we trailed along the Marais des Cygnes, the Middle Creek, the Sugar, the Osage, the Marmathon [sic], and even among the hazelbrush of Paint Creek: memory! . . . Soon after the retreating Ruffians had left our northern counties and actually did Peace reigned [sic] there the old free state party proper separated and struggles became visible for mere party voting, blinded by personal ambition & the hope of Party rewards. . . .[2]

An underlying source of this trouble in southeast Kansas was land and the fact that free-staters who had been driven off their claims during 1856 were now returning and trying to recover those claims.[3] As these claims and counterclaims grew the pro-slavery men sought justice in the courts and the free-state men felt they would be "unable to secure justice in the regular courts,"[4] the regular courts being the ones in Fort Scott which were controlled by pro-slavery men. The option the free-staters chose was to set up a court of their own, called the Squatter's Court.

In a letter in January, 1859, James Montgomery stated that a land claim case involving a dispute between Southwood and Stone had been the commencement of the trouble.[5] In September, 1856, a man named William Stone claimed he was driven off his claim and later forced to sign a bill of sale. His cabin was then occupied by a man named Southwood. In June of 1857 Stone returned to his claim and his friends helped him build another cabin on the same claim, so he could contest his rights to the land. An altercation occurred between their wives at the water well and Mrs. Southwood dangerously beat Mrs. Stone. Aroused by this violent act, dozens of Stone's friends drove Southwood off the claim. Later, accounts relate that Southwood turned up in Fort Scott before a grand jury and had the citizens who had ordered him off indicted for rebellion. It was this incident, according to Montgomery, that began the "new era" of trouble and Welch (1977) believed was an outgrowth of a "Wide Awake Society" that was formed soon after the attack on Mrs. Stone.[6]

The Squatter's Court, an instrument the free-state forces hoped to give them legal standing, was organized sometime in the late summer of 1857 but little information is known about it. The court met at the home of Oliver P. Bayne, "a large log house on the Osage river, built by John Brown and Captain Bain, near where the old Military Road between Fort Scott and Leavenworth crosses the Little Osage River."[7] Andreas (1883) lists Dr. Gilpatrick, of Anderson County, as judge and Henry Kilbourn, sheriff. In his report to the territorial legislature James Lane stated, "Colonel Abbott, Dr. Gilpatrick and the Rev. J. E. Stewart, . . . had been ordered there, arrived, and proceeded to establish a Squatter's Court for the redress of grievances and restoration of peace.[8]

Who actually was sheriff seems to be in question. Leonhardt wrote, "The Squatter's Court [was] established by Dr. Gilpatrick as Judge presiding, Rev. John E. Stewart Atty. for the prosecution, Col. Abbott as Atty. for the Defense. Clerk of Court & Sheriff any one that was willing to serve. . . .[9] Whether or not this was Leonhardt's humor shining through, Stewart was obviously the one that was employed to be the enforcer for the court.

James Hanway, a resident of Lane, Kansas, related an account that also mentions Gilpatrick and Stewart, as they had stopped at his house to eat:

> My wife began to ask some leading questions. Dr. Gilpatrick, who had been intimately acquainted with the family for years replied. "No questions must be asked." The request was obeyed, but every member of the family wondered the more "what does all this mean." A hasty breakfast was prepared and the party sat down to the table. From the back of each chair the navy revolvers were suspended by a belt. My wife laying her hand on the revolvers on the chair occupied by the "fighting preacher" Stewart, remarked:
>
> "We are told in scripture to entertain strangers, for thereby we may entertain angels unawares, but I would not suppose angels would carry with them such instruments of destruction as these." The 'fighting preacher' dropped his knife and fork, and turning half around in his chair, replied: "Madam, if they traveled in Kansas, they would soon find it was necessary."
>
> This breakfast party was the "squatter's court" organized to arbitrate the contested claims of Linn and Bourbon counties.
>
> J. H.[10]

In a different sketch Leonhardt related the Squatter's Court had Col. James B. Abbott as sheriff and "every man under Montgomery special Deputy sheriffs."[11] He also corroborated Robley's (1894) account concerning which book was used to swear in witnesses instead of the Bible, noting "the Squatters Court had no bible but had found somewhere in a _____ house a book known as Dr Gunns Physician and at another house a still more ludicrous work of a religious class _____ work of god man & the Devil this latter famous book the Defendants had now to kiss believing it to be the bible."[12]

In what is believed by the author to be the only known descriptions of cases tried at the Squatter's Court, other than the Beason case mentioned in Holloway's *History of Kansas*, Leonhardt gave us these details:

> A few important cases in this court I Beason. Hog Case 3 slaughtered hogs in open court confiscated to pay court fees. Money fine of $300 the team was taken as pay, prisoner released II Cary, David v/s Adkins, james Replevin of stock. Verdict Return his 3 yoke of cattle & pay for their use in breaking some proslavery mans prairey. Execution issued and all his stock taken to defray court & other expenses. Deft discharged. III Brunner, Alex v/s Galbray, Hughes Keeping Ruffians Hotel & Stolen goods. Verdict confiscation of all his property & ordered to leave the territory on pain of Death.18 witnesses sworn for the Prosecution & 10 for Defense. 4) Baily, Wm v/s Johnson, Peter Claim Dispute for R_____ stock. Verdict Restoration of all goods & chattels and a money fine of $200.00 for his use of thesame [sic]. . . . The most significant feature of the squatter court was that while it had an unliminet [sic] jurisdiciton it always moved into the Neighborhood of these Defendants to effect a speedy trial. . . .[13]

It was this court and the free-state settlers' attempts to circumvent the courts at Fort Scott that brought on the next confrontation between free-state and pro-slavery forces. Trouble began in December of 1857, although there is a discrepancy about the exact dates. One source of the trouble was a continuance of the Southwood-Stone dispute where, according to the *Herald of Freedom*, Southwood was arrested for threatening Mrs. Stone. After her husband was arrested Mrs. Southwood went to Fort Scott and asked the authorities there to help her gain his release. The Deputy Marshall, J. H. Little, raised a posse of 30 or 40 men and went to Bayne's place, but after his arrival there, he gave notice to disband. Failing to make any arrests for want of numerical strength, the marshal and his posse returned to Fort

Scott.[14] The wording of this indicates that a strong force of free-state men were already there if the marshal's posse of 30 or 40 was not strong enough to make any arrests, and this event took place before any calls for help were issued by free-state men.

At the same time, a man, possibly Southwood or someone else, had escaped from the Squatter's Court and attempted to make it to Fort Scott. The court's sheriff, John Stewart, and two men rode to intercept him but were themselves captured and taken into Fort Scott.[15] Stewart was held 10 days and posted bail but the other men refused bail and were held longer.[16] August Bondi, a free-state, Austrian emigrant to Kansas who had lived in Lane and Greeley, related that he and a group of men answered the call for help and left Greeley December 1, reaching Bayne's place on the Little Osage on December 2.[17] Bondi's account doesn't fit the accepted dates for the action unless for some reason they got an earlier call. However, from the wording of the first action it indicates a strong force of men was already there.

Either way, the call for help reached Lawrence sometime in early to mid-December, 1857, that the free-staters in and around the Squatter's Court needed help. General Lane, who would be authorized as major-general of the 1st Kansas Militia in a few days hence by the newly elected territorial legislature, tried to decide what do. He sent General W. A. Phillips to Fort Bayne, as it was soon being called, to let the men there know more help would soon follow.

> To Genl W. A. Phillips
>
> You will repair without delay to Sugar Mound
> and communicate with our friends who are there
> it is understood defending themselves against an
> invading force.
>
> J. H. Lane Maj. Genl.[18]

Probably Lane knew his military authorization was in the works and he was only waiting for its authorization before he went himself. Bondi, in his account of the fight that erupted there when Marshall Little and his men returned, said that "About 3 o'clock p.m., the Missourians came on to within 50 yards, when they spread out in open order and began firing; we replied, the action lasted an hour. The Missourians lost some horses and about ten men wounded, three of whom died in a few days. None of us received a scratch. During the engagement Col. Wm A. Phillips, the New York Tribune correspondent, came up on a gallop, hitched his horse under the upper river bank and jumped into our fortification. . . ."[19] This account corroborates the fact that Phillips went south early, but as mentioned, probably not as early as Bondi relates. Other accounts of the battle state between two and four of Little's posse were wounded but none died.[20] Leonhardt, who had in the last few days just returned to Lawrence from his trip back east, later wrote:

> "Two days before leaving Lawrence General Lane had ordered me to proceed to the front and report to him the state of affairs there. Rumors of renewed hostilities in Linn, Lykins,* & Bourbon counties had reached him. By the time I was prepared to do so, he himself came to my quarters at the Whitney House informing me both of us should ride together. Mr. E. B. Withman, [sic] the partner of Surveyor Searle went also with us, robed [sic] with the promised commission of Lane's Chief of Staff. This Withman [sic] was a sharp speculator and a well paid watchman in the service of the New England Aid Company. Pomeroy and Chs. H. Bronscomb [sic] were watched by Charles F. Conway, and all three were watched by this Withman. It takes certainly a rogue to watch a rogue!"[21]

On December 16, 1857, at an extra session of the newly elected free-state territorial legislature, Lane was authorized as major-general of the 1st Kansas Militia with the ability to commission officers.[22] Based on these new appeals for help, Lane proceeded to go south and make a show of force. That this was not a split-second decision is evident by Lane's order to General Phillips several days before Lane left. From Leonhardt's account, it even appears Lane thought first about sending Leonhardt instead of Phillips.

Leonhardt wrote that "Lane deemed it essential and politic _____ military glory to our men in the field by a visit to them and a grand inspection of those great army corps on paper."[23] Whatever the case, members of the Squatter's Court had asked for help in their problems with Fort Scott and Lane's order to Phillips followed by the ride south to enroll the militia was his response.

On the way south on December 17 or 18, according to Leonhardt, Lane and his staff stopped at the new town of Ohio City in Franklin County, and there Leonhardt was officially initiated into the secret Order of the Danites by General Lane himself:

Brother Mallory, now of the City of Lawrence was the grandmaster at the time when General James H. Lane received my oath which installed me a working member. It was at a farmhouse near the then hopeful paper burgh "Ohio City."* With the most sinister face he unsheathed his sword, made me place my left hand on it while I held my right arm up, he uttered these words. "are you willing and ready to assist in settling the great question of the Day? do you pledge obedience to carry out any order given you? Can you give up your life in making Kansas a free state? And do you solemnly swear never to recognize the bogus laws?" Had I not been years ago familiar with equal scenes that preceeded [sic] the joining of this Lodge I might have felt a little squemish [sic] about the subject matter. To each and all questions proposed I replied. "General, while I emphatically Say Ay! Ay! to all the questions put I do not recognize [the] necessity of this order in the least. When I left for Kansas, I had settled all these questions in my mind, but, if a record of the same is wanted I repeat Ay! Ay! And thus I urge you let us have less talkings [sic] and more doings around this great cause we have on our hands." Many others were initiated there.²⁴

Although this oath described by Leonhardt is different than the one quoted earlier from the *Leavenworth Herald*, Leonhardt's oath must also have included some part about secrecy, because later in his life, as he was engaged in his writings, Leonhardt felt very strongly about getting releases from the men he wanted to write about and remarked, "The writer has spent much time and travelled [sic] considerable in order to have the personal aproval [sic] of those who were Actors. The _____ of these coworkers remarked that in as much as they were not afraid of doing certain things but had no objections of having it told & let their names go in Stray Leaves _____ _____ but not all have given this Approval or their present Domicil [sic] unknown."²⁵ Another explanation

---

*Leonhardt's information fits with what is known about Ohio City. At the time, Ohio City was a town located about 1¼ miles northeast of the present-day town of Princeton, Kansas. The town was begun in 1857 and became the first permanent county seat for Franklin County. It had big plans of growing into the dominant city for Franklin County, but those plans, like many other hopeful town sites in Kansas, failed to materialize. Leonhardt, in his writings, refers to several such speculative towns as paper burghs because they were big towns on paper only, but he has nothing good to say of the men behind selling speculative town lots at exorbitant prices. (For more details on Ohio City and Lane's connection, see notes in Appendix.)

for the difference may be that because Lane was now initiating members away from Lawrence, the oath may have been ad libbed by Lane, who was an excellent speechmaker off the cuff.

After this initiation into the ranks of the Danites, Leonhardt continued, "From Ohio City we proceeded to Ossawatomie [sic] and still farther south, where Lane held a great dress parade with the troops under Montgomery, Abbott, Shorr, [sic] and Stewart near the trading post and Sugar Mound. . . .[26]

Although Bondi's dates appear inaccurate, his account of Lane's enrolling the militia is noteworthy. "On the evening of the 14th we were ordered to break camp, Montgomery's, Jennison's and Bayne's companies sufficient to preserve order, and Gen. Lane further ordered all men to meet at the school house at midnight, where, after a short speech, he enrolled all present (about 150) as the first members of the Kansas Jayhawkers. He explained the new name in this wise [sic]: As the Irish Jayhawk with a shrill cry announces his presence to his victims, so must you notify the pro-slavery hell-hounds to clear out or vengeance will overtake them."[27] While this is a little early for the use of the word *jayhawker*, I find it interesting that Lane ordered camp broken, then the men to report at midnight to be enrolled, and I believe it was at this point he also swore them in as Danites! Leonhardt wrote in one outline that "the Prariey [sic] City Guards under Capt. Samuel L. Shorr [sic] & almost every man near & far [were] sworn into this second Ordre [sic] of the Danites."[28] Using this as a precedent, it strengthens the idea that Lane did enroll the militia at Sugar Mound as Danites. Holloway's (1868) passage on this same event, further strengthens my claim as he noted about Lane, "On the evening of the same day he disbanded it, ordering all the men to return to their homes, except the companies of Captains Montgomery and Baynes, who were to keep the field, and protect the citizens. He organized, at the same time, a lodge of the secret society, whose object was the destruction of the Lecompton Constitutional measure.[29]

Leonhardt was clear in his writings that the first order of Danites was the group that had been formed at Lawrence, but after the split in the Free-State party in December, 1857, he explained:

> General James H. Lane went silently to work on his assigned mission, to shape the logs into the future battering ram, that finally destroyed the works of Darkness. He organized the Militia. _____
> with this event was the forming of the second Order of the Danites

into workers. This order was created with two fold objects in view. 1st Mutual and effective protection since there was neither Law, nor protection obtainable for free state men in the bogus courts, 2nd to assure the execution of all warmeasures [sic] found necessary to keep slavery out of the territory. That such an Organization had to be introduced among those very men, who knew well and deeply felt that Eternal vigilance is the only prize of Liberty, ought not surprise the reader. Especially not when it became known that only those radical free state men could become a member who were known as minuit [sic] men, when close fighting had to superseed [sic] speechyfying [sic]. Thus it happened that the mere Hon politician eloquent or hungry item hunters for Eastern papers actually knew Nothing even of the Existence of our Order.[30]

Certainly if one believes Bondi's account, Lane is clearly instructing these new militia men to order pro-slavery men out of southeast Kansas, which is a point that has been debated in the activities that followed for the next six months.

James Legate wrote that the Danite organization had not much more than a year's duration. Although we now know this to be inaccurate, it appears certain the first Danite group in Lawrence was either taken over by Lane or he was organizing others, molding and steering them into his own secret storm troopers, should the need for that arise. Initiating new Danites not at Lawrence, but at Ohio City and possibly at Sugar Mound, leads one to believe Lane had already stepped away from the old leaders at Lawrence. Leonhardt wrote that after his own group broke away from Lane, he [Lane] still had lodges at Lawrence and Topeka.[31]

Lane summed up the trip south in his report to the territorial legislature on February 15, 1858, stating:

> Immediately after the adjournment of your special session, I repaired to the scene of action, sending Generals Phillips and Plumb in advance, to inform the people that a force of U. S. troops were moving in that direction. Accompanied by Generals Stratton, Whitman, Shore and Leonhardt,[†] I arrived at Sugar Mound, where the people were encamped, under the command of Col. J. B. Abbott. . . .

[†]Leonhardt is often referred to as colonel and only a few times as general. Lane's referral to him as general in this instance must be because of his appointment by Lane under the December 16, 1857 bill that created a military board, however Leonhardt is not listed as one of the brigadier generals in the *Annals of Kansas*, page 154.

On the evening the companies were to be disbanded, our scouts brought news that a company of U. S. troops were moving upon us with the avowed intention of attacking us. We immediately took position, intending, if possible, with honor, to avoid a conflict, but prepared to meet it successfully, if forced upon us. We remained in this position, thus taken, until we ascertained written assurances from Judge Williams that the Free-State prisoners would be protected and treated kindly. Peace being restored, we disbanded the command, retaining two companies in the field, some thirty men, with orders to protect the inhabitants. . . .[32]

It is also on this trip that Leonhardt makes a strange claim and tells one of the reasons that he began to change his opinion of Lane.

"After the usual preparation for the grand inspection had been carried out I endeavored to bring this motley crew of Kansas Crusaders into battle array."[33] Leonhardt continued:

that Lane had to spoil everything. Scarcely had he commenced to the last sound of the Order 'Attack Brigade' passed from his lips when he rode to the right _____ & saying in an undertone Joe give me a chew! During the revolution of Europe in 1848 I had beheld many a carriacture [sic] among the armed citizen but this picture here of the Chief Commander asking for a chew of tobacco was emphatically far ahead of anything my military eyes had ever witnessed.[34]

Leonhardt seemed shocked at Lane's slovenly breach of protocol and it was the beginning of what would sour him on Lane. He continued:

After inspection we formed ourselves into a quasi committee of the whole without anybody presiding over the August Body. We heard heart rendering reports of many cruelties of this new outbreak of the political cancer and the men were pleading with Lane to take to the field in person & hurl the foe back into Missouri. But he councilled [sic] them forebearance [sic] a little while longer . . . Montgomery and his men replied: "General we can't stand it a day longer, we must do it, even without you!" . . . Lane made many mistakes as a military leader. Here he committed a most serious one. Had he remained true to 'his Boys' and left political aspirations a little while longer untouched, the whole host of his opponents combined could have never outraced him![35]

Instead, Lane enrolled the militia and then dismissed them.

After Lane failed to authorize any action in Linn County, Leonhardt wrote that Montgomery took him aside and asked,

> "What is the matter with General Lane?" to which I remarked: I too do not understand him, unless it be that the men at Lawrence & Topeka deem it prudent to delay all troubles on the front till the Ellection [sic] next January is over. . . . "But sir I beg you to consider this very delay strengthens our foes, we must strike now, or certain as the sunshines [sic] . . . we loose the cause." Grasping his hand I replied, "Montgomery that is exactly my state of thinking. When you have retired to your different camps, let us reorganize our secret order and cut entirely loose from Lawrence."[36]

Leonhardt's use of the word *our* secret order leads one to believe that Montgomery was also in the Danites. It is interesting to note in this passage that it is Leonhardt who suggested that Montgomery's group break away from the Lawrence group.

Leonhardt's disappointment over inaction can be felt by his next lines. "We soon parted with the men from the border leaving everything not only in a very unsettled condition but still worse, like the king of France, we had only marched up the hill and thenn [sic] down again."[37]

On the way back from Sugar Mound, Lane and his staff stopped at Osawatomie and "Lane gave a fierce Warspeech at the drugstore."[38] Leonhardt again reflected on his disappointment with Lane and noted that after Lane's speech:

> I confess of having felt sad and morose. Neither Lane's speech, nor such extravgant [sic] superfluenties [sic] bestowed upon his mere words when I well knew what he failed to do only hours ago, could crowd down my utter disgust with the whole performance. . . . But I was not the only dissatisfied one in that meeting. Chs. Foster sprang to his feet and stated to his townsmen that the writer of these sketches was hiding himself [sic] behind the counter, and that meant something was awfully wrong at the front. . . . I said gentlemen, by the actions of our many delegates at different conventions assembled, General James H. Lane has become the commander in Chief of our free state forces in the whole territory. He is therefore your & my Leader. He has been trusted with the duties of enrolling our whole strength to protect the ballot boxes at the coming Ellection [sic] in January next. So far, but not farther, his duties are well defined. The enemy is again upon us, harming the houses of free state men, killing our brother on the front, committing again unheard of cruelties, but still it is the expressed opinion of General Lane, we must submit the right time to strike the foe, has not come yet. We all at

> the different camps differ from his discission [sic] and must assume all responsibilities for ourselves in order not to marr his future political prospects. Harken unto me, the men of Ossawatomie [sic]. Leader or no Leader, the men on the border are ready to strike the blow most any moment. And twice woe be to all political Demagogues who fetter hand & foot of General Lane to lead us on at once. But fight we must, come what will, gentlemen I speak for myself and in behalf of those very men, we left behind us only a few hours ago![39]

Although Leonhardt clearly disagreed with Lane's decision not to make an attack on behalf of the men of Linn County he worded his speech very carefully as a way of putting no responsibility on Lane or damaging Lane's future political career.

On the ride back to Lawrence the next day, after leaving Captain Shore and Whitman at Prairie City, Leonhardt related a conversation he had with Lane:

> Do you know that I actually have the best change [sic] of being the next president of the nation? Why not general, my reply, There was such a man as Franklin Pierce with whom all had to ask each other who is he? Your call is vastly different. You have already earned a world wide renown & fame. Why should you fail in taking hold of one of those many, nay, the uppermost rolling waves that are just now _____ dashing headlong in the boisterous political storm and ride triumphantly over into the white house. But dear general, with the poor sinner on Golgatha Heights, I would humble murmur: remember me when you are in that political paradise. In that event sir consider yourself the future Consul general to most any court of Europe, Lane promised! . . . Completely overcome with the promise of such undreamed of distinction I bowed my head in submission to the coming fate. . . .[40]

Although in this exchange Leonhardt played along with Lane, he admitted it bothered him that Lane would make such a political promise so easily. After they returned to Lawrence Leonhardt continued, "My clever roommate E. D. Ladd was just holding justice court in that little white frame house near the Eldridge House. . . . The more I contemplated upon past events, the more convinced I became that General Lane was already placing himself on the incline plain [sic] downwards and might unknown to himself slide off. Of one point I was certain, Lane had for Ever lost hold of the heart of one of his former Boys!"[41]

Chapter 4 Into the Epicenter

If one believes Leonhardt's dates to be accurate then the next series of events would have had to have happened very quickly. Most sources agree, and Lane himself wrote that he went south to enroll the militia in Linn County on December 17, 1857, which would put their return to Lawrence around December 23. Leonhardt wrote:

> Census returns beyond doubt, our party had the greatest number of actually [sic] settlers and our triumph at the January Ellection [sic] became certain provided always, our friends of Missouri would stay at home. But the recent moves of Brockett, [and] Clark, Ruffian Leaders threatened again our prospects. These fellows became very daring and many reports reached Lawrence of their depredations. Many writers for Eastern papers did repeatedly ask me, if I would hasten to the front and stop the fuss. . . . I kept my own counsil [sic]. But when Affaina Johnson, the noble minded minister of that tribe of Indians had succeeded in getting the dispatch from Montgomery to me, that I was wanted at his camp, I concluded to start at once to move. I told my errand, except to R. J. Hinton an extreem [sic] Radical young Englishmen who too wrote for some Eastern paper. . . . I met with Montgomery & his men near the trading post, Stewart‡ & his men were on picket duty a few miles south east of there.[42]

---

‡Stewart, after being taken prisoner near Fort Scott, was held 10 days and reported released, so Stewart could have been back on this date.

5

The Danites in Action

At this point in the action, Leonhardt noted it "was thought proper among the 'fighting Kansans' . . . that the 'wheat must be separated from all chaff.' Just now somebody introduced a new 'thrasher' and 'separator' for that kind of work. Who the Patentor actually was I failed to learn. That much I do know, it could not have been a calculating Yankee, because of the unheard of generosity for everybody to use and improve upon that same machinery at will. The Secret Order of 'the Kansas Danites owned the Territorial Rights.'"[1] In using this terminology, Leonhardt admitted he didn't know where the term came from, but Blackmar (1912) gave us the answer in his description of the Mormon Danites. After being called the Destroying Angels, the Mormon band took the name of the Big Fan, "whose duty was to separate the chaff from the wheat."[2]

In a noteworthy analogy relating pro-slavery settlers to weeds, Leonhardt described the situation this way:

> Captain James Montgomery send [sic] word. There must be some weeding done in his section of the country at once as all these obnoxious weeds had become fully ripe and might throw out their seeds. As a humble husbander he much feared that one year of each seeding would cause us many a year of hard weeding. On my road down south I concluded to use the new Thrasher and Separator as we had several assortments of different sized riddles according the specific "growth" to be separated from the weeds![3]

It would appear that Leonhardt and these Danites, under the leadership of Montgomery and Stewart, had now broken from the Danite lodge in Lawrence, but exactly when this split actually occurred is hard to determine. In a newspaper article written in 1878, Leonhardt said that the three of them, Montgomery, Stewart, and himself, worked on their

> own responsibility in Linn and Johnson counties. These events occurred after we Danites had been forced to secede from the Grand Lodge of Lawrence, on account of the great stupidity of our high

priests and others of the Lodge who did no other work but to hold offices at their headquarters in Lawrence. . . . [Lane] held the leading strings for a while. But when it came to pass that he assumed the role of Dictator, saying in open Lodge: "It matters but little what this or that man's political preference might be, the main point to consider is this: Is he a Lane man?" Then and there even the mighty brother Lane lost his hold and control of all the thinking members of our Lodge, and seceding border brethren knew him no more.[4]

Leonhardt related that he had gone south and met up with Montgomery and Stewart and noted that "under the Danite Reorganization . . . James Montgomery, John Stewart, and himself had charge of actions. . . . We changed grips, signs and passwords."[5] The first action they took, and one Leonhardt wrote "was his own planning,"[6] was against a man named Van Sumbeux.* "This rascal," Leonhardt noted, "had killed three free State men and had been very conspicuous in plundering Ossawatomie [sic],"[7] We pick up the story in Leonhardt's own words:

> After a prolonged consultation with Montgomery & Stewart the following plans of operation were given to our Brother Danites for immediate aproval [sic]. 1st to leave off, defending ourselves, but attack the enemy at different points at the same time. 2nd Avoid if possible a general conflict with Missourians. 3rd Compell every proslavery man in the border, who harbored Ruffians to leave. 4th Kidnapping a negro should be punished with death. The troops U. S. at fort scott should be coaxed to come out and follow one of our parties, while the other should dart into it and bring some prominent proslavery men as hostages in camp to compell citizens of fort scott to keep peace with us. future Events will prove how well the plans did work. When the men were asked shall we unchain the dogs of war all voted yea! And now to some of the work. A few miles down the little Osage lived that human fiend and murder [sic] of several free state men Vansumbuex or Zumkault? Thesame [sic] who put first the torch to the Dwellings of Osawatomie. He was a desperado from the plains out west. Our scouts would occasionally find a written notice posted to the effect, that the Yankees were cordially invited to call at his house and take tea with him & his many friends. After I had read one

---

*This name is also spelled by Leonhardt as Van Sumbolt, Zamalt by the *Herald of Freedom*, May 8, 1858, and Zumkault by John Holloway (1868).

of thesame [sic] posters myself, I considered this man the great Leader of his clans and to take him alive was our highest ambition. Montgomery's statement fully convinced me, this man was of great note among the proslavery neighbors.

Our plans to make the first call on Vansumbolt were soon perfected. We knew that he was hardly ever without a host of Ruffians camping in his timber. I examined their campfire myself and could have easily thrown a stone into their camp kittles. I knew the whole place. We succeeded in pushing a strong force of footmen into the timber, between the loghouse and the former camp of the ruffians. A ficticious note had been sent them to be on the lookout for the yankees at the lower crossing near Burns place. They left in great glee. We had half of the battle won. And now quick boys to work. It is almost daylight. Stewart had selected for this nice piece of work: Buchanan, Pickles, Coppock, Dick Pearson, Eliza Hill, Archer Candrell, & R. J. Hinton, Montgomery, Pat Devlin, Cleveland & two others whose names I lost from my daybook. We had surrounded the house and felt consciously for any loopholes, found several of them. As they could only be removed from the inside we placed our rifles in such a position that they were able to do terrible work, in case of enemies being inside. About twenty feet from the door and directly opposite was the well & smokehouse. Montgomery placed himself there to cover the door and fire the moment the writer should either be shot by the outcoming foe, or Vansumbeux should succeed doging [sic] my ball. Hinton's special duty was, as soon as the door should be opened and but one shot fired, to force his way into the cabin, kick the backlog in the fireplace to give us more light on the subject. And this smart young Englishman did all that with a coolness which best spoke of his strong nerves of steel! I know of many a stallwart [sic] Kansan especially is that true, among those very man who were ever anxious to belittle him who would have utterly failed us, where they asked to stand Now in Mr. Hinton's place here to my left. My right hand grasped firmly the revolver while knocking at the door. "Who's thare"[sic]—a woman's voice spoke. "We have business with Mr. Vansumbolt," my reply. "Who are you D. What do you want." "The avenging Danites have called on you to give an account for the murder of our men. Are you ready to entertain your guests. It is your last tea party." A few heinous oaths, and all was still. I strained every nerve that constitute clear perception but perceived only a sly kreeping [sic] along the floor of one person. All at once the door opened before I even had ascertained which way this opening would occur and so close came his fowling piece to my head a long Kentucky rifle, that I had to lean sidewards. He fired at me. The ball send [sic] my spectacles, though fastened by a strong rubber band to regions unbenowest [sic] the ball went through the brim of my black felt hat. Montgomery's rifle spoke next, his ball almost grasing [sic] my left ear, breaking Vansumbolt's right collarbone the ball went clear through and lodged in a log. R. J. Hinton jumped over the body of the fallen foe now lying halfway in the door and cooly kicked the backlog, as if but trying to warm his cold feet. I sprang also in the room and requested the woman to make no noise or suffer the consequences. We propted [sic] the ugly looking big hole in our foes chest. The following questions were asked by Montgomery: "Where is the powder & lead you have stored away? Quick man answer or instant death is your penalty." He hesitated for some time, but feeling the prope [sic] being removed by Montgomery, and bleeding profusely, he at last confessed. Several kegs of powder and I think about fifty pounds of lead in bars we threw into the creek being too bulky and dangerous for us to transport to our camp. Our men were determined to kill the varmin as Pat Devlin called him. Some men for hanging him, a few to suffer him to bleed to death. But better counsil [sic] prevaileth. It was agreed to make him the very first person whom we ordered to leave for Missouri inside of twenty-four hours or suffer certain death by order of the Danites. He promised faithfully to leave if we but would spare his Life! He did leave. . . .[8]

In his book *A History of Kansas*, Holloway also described the shooting of Van Zumkault but claimed it took place in February, 1858.[9] Apparently Holloway used as his source the articles in the Lawrence newspaper. These were published usually several months after the fact and were written by a source that called himself "Cherokee."[†]

Leonhardt continued with his accounts of their actions:

From here we called on the older farry[‡] the next obnoxious proslavery man of the neighborhood. We reached his house just as the family was about ready to pertake [sic] of their breakfast. Our hungry men enjoyed that breakfast most certainly. I informed farry that he had to leave for Missouri next day or suffer immediate death after the expiration of that period. He was very willing to go. We needed Blankets

---

[†]The identity of the writer known as "Cherokee" is unknown, but Montgomery said Cherokee's articles were "remarkably accurate." *Lawrence Republican*, Jan. 20, 1859.

[‡]The *Herald of Freedom,* May 8, 1858, had this pro-slavery family's name spelled as Farris.

& Quilts. Here were many useless stored away. Those of us who needed some, helped themselves. All these orders to leave were now given by the order of the Danites. at the farry's house we found a little negro boy of about a year old, lying naked in front of the fireplace, warming his self [sic]. After our men had almost finished their breakfast, Joe Coppock took the little chap in his arm, put him on the table and made him dance into the meatplate under a shower of laughter of all the men, except its natural father. Montgomery brought the young slave mother of that boy to me and said: "Sir, this poor creature, does not want to be free, she would rather go back with her master into Missouri." We did not coerce her into freedom. To several more places we went on that day bringing messages from the reorganized order of the Danites. At noon on the following day the new era of "mowing back" into Missouri took place, by order of the Kansas Danites. We went near fort scott and drove several of the most obnoxious neighbors with equal success back to Missouri, by order of the Danites. Written orders were issued & fastened to outhouses of others. to leave and all this by order of the Danites. *example of order—Leave for Missouri never return! If found in _____ _____ _____ from date, you shall suffer the penalty _____ many crimes. . . .

We made our movements quickly and with telling blows. Our little Army not quite two hundred men strong was detached in small forces, we would all meet at certain rendezvous and when morning came, we were perhaps twenty miles away. Our Army became thus greatly exacerately [sic] by our foes and soon we learned the startling news from a fugitive slave who had found our camp, that the whole free state Army under Jim Lane, a thousand strong shall come and harry every proslavery hunter! His army had already driven every hunter from the south fork of Middle Creek clean down to fort scott! This slave had fled from his hunter only a few miles south of our camp. He was in terrible fear of being ove_taken by a slave hunter with his two bloodhounds that were on his trail. We listened with great sympathy to his many tales of the deepest dies of cruelty. There was a new feature for all of us abolitionists before us. To face the manhunter and his bloodhounds. I fail to describe our exact state of idignation [sic]. Before long the hounds came in our camp. A shot or shumping [sic] up and that dog had traced the last slave! Its owner was also overtaken _____ by the slave and delt [sic] with according to the stern rules of our order. He was a professional slavehunter and was hung by a jurry [sic] of his countrymen![10]

Although Welch (1977) believed that Montgomery had retired from the field and used Holloway (1868) as his source,[11] a careful reading of Holloway does not bear this out. In fact, Holloway says just the opposite. Writing about the event he noted, "After this occurrence [the shooting of Van Zumkault] Montgomery proposed to retire from the field."[12] Leonhardt's account corroborates Holloway's but appears to be wrong on its date for the shooting; in addition, other sources substantiate the February date.

I believe it is possible that Leonhardt, writing of the event years later, did confuse his dates and that the shooting of Van Zumkault occurred in February of 1858. Leonhardt went south from Lawrence at least four different times and may have confused which event happened on which trip. Leonhardt mentioned in his account that he carried a daybook and in a different manuscript noted later, "I have traveled on the historic border for the sole purpose to meet with former associates and compare my fieldnotes."[13] I doubt too many other men involved in the border troubles carried a daybook in which they took notes, which should add some credence to Leonhardt's accounts.

My attempt to link the Danites as being the original Jayhawkers begins here. No organized group during the Bleeding Kansas era, other than John Brown's, had attempted to stay in the field on a continual mission of harassment, and as this group did exactly that, they set the precedent that followed and became the Jayhawkers in late 1858. It was the decision to turn the Danites into an action group that set this in motion.

As mentioned previously, other written sources give the account for the shooting of Van Zumkault in February, 1858. Leonhardt gave it as Christmas Day, 1857, and stated that had been the beginning day for the Danites' new mission of forcing pro-slavery settlers out of southeast Kansas. He noted they were doing this as a way to prepare for the upcoming election on January 4, 1858. It was this election that would decide which constitution Kansas would attempt to join the Union with. Leonhardt claimed that the free-staters had to know whether or not the pro-slavery forces in Missouri were planning on crossing into Kansas again and attempt to control the election through fraudulent voting means. This was the purpose behind their action, or canvassing, to go into Missouri and find this out, all before the election and hopefully to prevent it.

"Certain it is," wrote Leonhardt, "that had the reorganized order delegated its work in Linn, _____ and Bourbon County in fall & winter of 1857 there would have been a large invasion of volunteer voters at the January Ellection [sic]. Though none of us working Danites has thus far proven his superiority in forseen [sic] future and become a Master politician, neverless [sic] certain, credit is Due to those who furnished Brains for this new Departure in the order of the Danites. They hurled not only successfully the straggling Ruffian tenants back into Missouri, but their late Landlords likewise."[14]

After driving out some of the pro-slavery settlers Leonhardt related:

> We retreated back to our former quarters near the trading post. Our fair [sic] here was pretty tough. We were out of most everything. At last a great change occurred. flour & bacon found its way to camp. Granaries also. We boarded at the house of some so called free state man, as long as the provisions lasted. It was here where Washington Buchanan uttered that much commended upon prayer at the supper table. This Buchanan was a jovial fellow, always ready for any emergency. No matter what that might be. He had been out scouting while the new provisions had come in and knew nothing of their existence, till called for supper. Coming in, he saw happy faces all around & smell [sic] perhaps the perfum [sic] of the cooking & lacking provisions, but still had doubts who might become the envied partakers of these good things. We set to the table. It had been prepared by some of the men to take Buchanan by surprise. Our new Lady presided at on_end [sic] of the table. One of the uppermost jesters in that crowd bowed his head and solemly [sic] said. Brother Wash. please ask the usual blessings of our camps. We looked at each other, but saw fit to fasten our eyes on the plates before us, waiting coming events. In well bekoning [sic] melodious words the response came:
>
> > "O Lord be tho for ever praised!
> > Behold how utterly all here amazed!
> > We thank thee that things at last have changed.
> > Hot biscuit and pure tea
> > for supper again we see,
> > Where formerly only corndodgers
> > And field Beans were intended.
>
> Horror stricken the old Lady said afterwards to her man. Lor' me, them thare fellers mus be wors' un than heathen Injuns.[15]

Leonhardt's humorous musings continued:

> At another occasion we had strayed into the house of a southern born free state man from whom we got dinner for ourselves & horses. He was paid by an order on the territorial executives the necessary papers were signed & countersigned with the very name of proslavery militia man, but written in pencil. When the would be quartermaster handed him these documents saying, "Keep these papers till the tax gatherer from Lecompton comes and you may pay your taxes with it." I do not know if that man could read what was written, but he did say, "Look a here, boys, I was told at the store sich are writings had arter be in pen and ink." Correct friend, the quarter master replied, but you see I am out of ink, You just give it to the Post master and he can copy it. Can't he write? to be sure, he is an awful right smart kind of a man "that idiots reply."[16]

Although Leonhardt wrote these reflections with humor in mind, they illustrate what the Danites were up to, and they show the Danites were serious about finding out if the Missourians were planning to cross over and vote. Along that line Leonhardt continued:

> At the close of 1857 a flank movement into Missouri was contemplated by the working Danites at the border. All attempts to draw the U. S. troops out of fort scott had failed. Either they had received orders to let us alone, or some fears had made themselves felt, that the men under Montgomery would certainly fight the troops, if fired upon first. The Ellection [sic] in January next was at our very door. We felt that we owed our friends over the line a visit in becoming style, as they had made us so many. If our scouts had reported correctly, there would be no invasion in the northern counties. The only road by which such a swarm would likely come, was through Bourbon county. Captain Stewart's company was chosen for the raid into Missouri. His men where [sic] almost entirely strangers to the Missourians, properly speaking while Montgomery's men lived closer to the line. Our object in this raid was twofold. To fill our entirely empty larders on the home trip and play Missourians on their way to Kansas in order to ascertain the feelings among her people in regard to the coming ellection [sic]. We had splendid success in both. We ventured fully 20 miles over the Line by different roads, all of which had been maped [sic] out before we started by different scouts. Montgomery & his men were chosen to act as reserve in case of disaster and came close up to the state boundary for that purpose. Kansas Danites has a

signed corps of their own invention. Had our advance run into the Missourians we would have fought while falling back till our reserves were ready to receive us. Their fire arms could not compete with ours and they well knew that. When we had reached a certain cross road, the axis of our flank movement, we concluded to get dinner at a large double loghouse. The honored Jeremiah Clark resided there. He was the so called bell whether [sic] among the roughest Ruffians. We ellected [sic] him for his notorious proslavery sentiments. He had been over in Kansas to vote several times that was reported & he was certainly a fit subject to interview in regards to the coming ellection [sic]. With a little arrangements among ourselves at the start, we actually did look like respectable Missourians on their way for Kansas to vote. We saluted the owner of the plantation with real southern behavior and inquired: Have the boys got here yet neighbor? Could they have taken the wrong trail? Heard any news about them yankees that are cutting H __ across the Line? Heard anything? No! Yes I doss. Our boys on the big prairy left an hour b'fore sun to join Col. Joe Turner's boys somewhere near fort scott.

Mr. Clark had by this time come out on the road and he began to introduce us. Charley White, alias Pickles, Joe Coppock & Stewart were the chieftains that had the honor of being questioned. "How many you uns be thare coming to help settle the hash for them bl— b yankees?" Don't know xactly how many thare might be we uns when all turn out, them that is true to our noble cause. Thare be a right smart heap of we-uns fighting boys. Chs Pickles uttered. "Well, I declare, had you boys rather slide & get a bite such as we have you uns are welcome. Come right smart way down the ribber I spose, ain't it a glorious work to secure the sacred rights of the South?" Our scouts performed well their parts. We did slide and soon our horses feasted on oats still yet in bundles, which we preferred to hay before feeding corn. We formed ourselves in different groups. One part of us did most of the talking, the majority was in helpless dilemma, bashful and greatly embarrassed fearing all the time our pronounciation [sic] would betray us. Dinner was announced, though room at the table only for half our number. And for even this mishapp [sic] we had made our prior arrangements. We had mixed among the many embarrassed a few of our fluent talkers in southern saings [sic]. Our dinner was to us a fest indeed! Spare ribs shank bones well roasted, fried sausages with excellent "taters" _____ butter & a real tread [sic] corncakes & honey. But a very laughable farce happened at the table. Oh that I had the power of giving the Reader a correct idea of that illiterate patriotic southern woman, who presided _____ our feast, thundering her philippica [sic] of unceasing hate for you men of Kansas! said she: "Now boys, when you uns get thare to Lawrence try to catch me Jim Lane, that vile sone of perdition he ain't fit to live anyhow. Kill every abolitionist. Oh, how I does hate them. I know them well. I do say, I can smell them critters a mile of[f]." to which Coppock responded: "How do they look anyhow?"

Having just helped Stewart to another piece of apple pie, I gave him a kick with my foot and asked. "how do you like that Captain?" To which he replied, taking a forkful: "oh that's nice, was never treaded [sic] to such before!" looking towards that woman, who smiled at his flattery. We all understood the mutual misunderstanding. Matters grew from bad to worse. A few left the table saying thei're [sic] horses needed attention. But scarcely had they been at the feedlot, they rolled among the straw, throwing bundles of oats at each other. Happy, _____ happy fellows that could open their safety valves in hearty laughter. Dinner over we went out on the porch facing the road, but even here we did not dare to look at each other in the face. Nature did not put much "Laugh" in the making of my humble selve [sic]. Though my capacities by storing away many a sidesplitter are very few & far between, but, should there ever again happen equal scenes, "Laugh" I will even knowing well I had to fight afterwards! A real hearty laugh, one that upsets the waterworks in both of your eyes, is the healthiest exercise for both old & young. When our horses were brought out they looked fresh & rested. We had a hard ride before us to hunt up Colonel Joe Turner on his road for fort scott. Mr. Clark was called for his bill. He looked strangely agitated and made the remark, that he had fed many a man & his horse while going to do the work in whipping Kansas to reason, but had never asked for pay. Stewart stepped forward & calling the Landlady to come out on the porch in bitter words said: "Well neighbor, this time your nostrils played a bad trick, we are not what you took us to be, Missourians, but real genuine Kansas Abolitionists. We came to warn you & your friends to stay away from Kansas. Did you ever see such fire Arms among your men? These are H. Ward Beecher's Bibles my man, & here are a few New Testaments from up north. We warn you & your friends in time. Did you hear of the new free state troops, that are ready any moment to cross to Missouri, if you should dare to send your men to Kansas. We here are a part of the Army of Kansas Danites! The bill sir, if you please. With you we make an exception, we will neither press nor jayhawk anything from you this time." ten dollars paid for our feast which the trembling man accepted, while his better half opened wide her eyes but spoke nothing. Lot's wife must have looked like her! We parted, all had learned something. Of the many laughters among us that followed even long after this event, there was no end. Whenever times became dull in camp, some of the very men would be getting up subscription papers for a dinner party at Clarkes Restaurant in the good state of Missery [sic]. Fifteen eventful years have since passed away, leaving mane [sic] vacant places among that social Dinnerparty.[17]

This is quite a story. As previously mentioned, the humor is obvious, but the historical context is important to illustrate just what the Danites were up to as well as the fact that the fear of an invasion of Missouri voters was a real threat to the contemporaries of the day. Referring back to the "separating the wheat" terminology, Leonhardt summed up this series of events by saying "the new era of mowing back to Missouri had begun."[18]

The election on January 4, 1858, took place without a pro-slavery victory. Leonhardt didn't say where he and Reverend Stewart were, but accounts relate that Montgomery destroyed the ballot box at Sugar Mound after finding out the true case on the ballot.[19]

Also around the beginning of January, a dead body turned up south of Lecompton, that of a man named Christ Kuntz. The following is the announcement in the *Herald of Freedom*, January 9, 1858:

> A German by the name of Kuntz was found dead near his residence several miles south of Lecompton a few days ago. He took a prominent part in the pro-slavery ranks during the troubles of 1856, and as the recollection of several dark deeds are associated with his name, it is not improbable that justice has been meted out to him by some of his old antagonists in rather a summary and unceremonious manner.[20]

This is an example of a deed done by the Danites that Leonhardt said remained behind the veil of contemporary knowledge. Leonhardt related the following account about this killing:

> Beyond the mere "Item" Disurbances on the border and Jayhawker abroad, nothing could be told the puplic [sic] as the Actors in such cases enjoined the fullest assistance of the strictest secrecy among themselves. We had no assassin in camp. Had certain men among the enemy be put to death, such was always with and under the consent of all. Those to whom the duty fell to execute such war measures were

but the Agents of the Rest. We always preferred to share all danger equally. James H. Lane knew well the meaning he exclaimed upon so many occasions—"oh but for the unwritten history of Kansas." The killing of Dutch Henry for instance belongs to that same unwritten page of history. Everybody was told this by some Newspaper, but no more. We will lift the veil. Dutch Henry had a claim on the Potawatomie Creek by Anderson Co/ franklin co. The crossing at his place was called after him. Though a German by birth, he had become very proslavery, was a fighter and among the Ruffians who undertook to capture John Brown and his men. At the battle of Osawatomie where Frederick Brown was killed our men lost also one man being captured. His name was Dutch Charley—He was also a German, a former subject of Austria and a fighter by choice with considerable experience. His full name was Charles Kaiser. Among the Ruffians in Camp was also a man by name of Chirst Kontz, [sic] another descendent of the otherwise so favorable race as friends of liberty, the teutonic. This Koontz was a very hard case when he became pro-slavery, he meant the whole thing of it. When the Ruffians in Camp held a counsil [sic] what to do with their Yankee prisoner, Koontz sprang to his feet exclaiming—"let the Dutch, kill the Dutch." He then commanded Dutch Henry to show his grit who only too soon sprang to his feet, walked towards the prisoner and deliberately shot Charles Kaiser dead through the head. . . . "Nat Humphrey" was furnished whiskey on a certain occasion and then told how they killed Dutch Charley. When this sad news reached camp our members became silent. None spoke. They looked into each other's eye. They all understood the order—to be on a keen lookout for the murder [sic] and his associates. Both men, Dutch Henry and Koontz were now by a rising vote in deep silence condemned to die. While out scouting after the victim James H. Almes and Archie Campbell overtook Billy Patterson and struck him. His name otherwise was Dutch Henry. John E. Stewart and Willitz Dorn [or Horn] found the other Billy Patterson and thus rid the world of Christ Koontz.[21]

Leonhardt noted that he and Stewart went to Lecompton at the end of January (see chapter 6) but then he must have returned to Lawrence. An "attack" was made against Fort Scott on February 11, 1858, by Montgomery and his men when they entered the town to serve writs against some pro-slavery men for the robbery of D.B. Johnson. The pro-slavery men that were wanted had simply fled into Missouri to return after Montgomery and his men left empty-handed.

Now "with rumors continually spreading to Kansas of the dire threats of retaliation . . . the subsequent return to Fort Scott of the border ruffians and the failure to return Johnson's property offered a fresh excuse to call for aid from Lawrence," the appeal made by Captain Bayne. "Bayne's appeal was heeded and prompted about fifty men to leave Lawrence for the seat of the trouble on February 24."[22] Leonhardt was the leader of this group of men and they took along a cannon.[23] In a later sketch, Leonhardt wrote of the event that "Montgomery sent for me and two pieces of Artillery, Sacramento§ & Betsy. I went [with] Richard J Hinton among John E Stewart's men & as my Aid de camp commanded our march on the little Osage first. Van Sumbolt was the first we visited."[24] With this passage, it appears Leonhardt contradicts his earlier statements that this happened before the end of 1857 and that he was indeed confused on his timing of the events. The main difference in the two versions is that earlier he said only he and Hinton went south and in the second account he led a group of men down. We don't know if Lane authorized this mission, but it may be Leonhardt was acting officially, since he was given the use of cannons. Welch wrote, "There is no evidence that the companies from Lawrence and Osawatomie were enrolled or connected with the territorial militia."[25] However, knowing that Leonhardt was in charge of this detachment from Lawrence and knowing Leonhardt's role and background with the Danites, as well as being Lane's adjutant, one can assume these men probably were connected with the territorial militia or the Danites, who according to Leonhardt, were generally one in the same. Whether or not they were under any orders from Lane is unknown.

Federal troops again were called out, this time on February 26, 1858, under the command of Captain George Anderson. Montgomery

---

§"Old Sacramento" was the nickname of the cannon captured by U.S. forces during the Mexican War and later taken to an arsenal in Missouri. Looted by Border Ruffians, it was taken to Kansas to help Ruffian forces. The cannon was at the town of Franklin near Lawrence, when free-state forces raided the town and captured the gun in August, 1856. It was used at the sack of Lawrence, Ft. Saunders, Titus, and Hickory Point. Leonhardt noted that Sacramento was at John E. Stewart's homestead, an Underground Railroad depot outside of Lawrence, in the spring of 1860, and was fired at pro-slavery raiders that attacked Stewart's place. This cannon is now believed to be the one on display at the Watkin's Community Museum of History in Lawrence.

may well have retired from the field temporarily, as noted by Welch, and his command assumed by Reverend Stewart. "Now . . . began a wholesale system of robbing, plundering and driving out of pro-slavery settlers."[26] According to Holloway (1868), it was at this time when Van Zumkault was shot, and a change in tactics was clear, a change Welch attributed to the possible change in command from Montgomery to Stewart.[27] If February, 1858, is the correct date for the shooting, but one believes Leonhardt's account about Van Zumkault, then that leads one to believe Montgomery had not retired from the field. Whatever the case, this change in tactics was clearly effective as the following extract from a letter written to Governor Denver, March 5, 1858, relates:

> Settlers are flying with their families to this plays [sic], leaving thier [sic] property behind. Scores are leaving [the] Osage valey [sic], daily, and fleeing to save their lives having received notices, of which, the following is a litteral [sic] copy, taken from one in my possession, which was taken from a settlers door, and brought to me by Captain Anderson.
> "Leave this claim in 24 hours."
> John Brown Capt_[28]

Why this notice would have been signed "John Brown" may only be surmised at this time.

The following extract from Captain Anderson's letter to Governor Denver substantiates the shooting of Van Zumkault as being in February:

> The second day after my arrival at this place (Feb 28) I accompanied the U. S. Deputy Marshall with 50 men as a posse to execute writs and disperse a body of marauders some 50 or 60 in number who were committing depredations on the Little Osage. . . . They had driven several men from their claims, robbed others of everything they possessed and shot one man, for an old grudge growing out of the difficulties of /56—I was informed by men of both parties that they boasted that they raised this foray, to draw me from Ft. Scott with all my men when they intended to sack the place and destroy it. . . . The aim of these marauders seems to be to drive the pro-slavery party out of this part of the country as all violence has so far been directed against men of that party, and in no instance has a man of the other party been molested.[29]

Indeed, Captain Anderson was correct, as that is exactly what Leonhardt said the Danites had in mind and corroborates one of Leonhardt's stated objectives. Holloway claimed the free-state men under Preacher Stewart, "after performing a few praiseworthy deeds, began plundering, robbing, and stealing, and running off the spoils to the north, and for this reason Montgomery reorganized his men and, re-entering the field, began to correct some of the wrongs committed. Preacher Stewart and some of his men proceeded north on a thieving expedition . . . were worsted in their unlawful attempts, and finally returned, the best of whom were reinstated in the original command."[30]

Things settled down somewhat for a few weeks and then on the night of March 27, 1858, a group of pro-slavery men stopped at the home of Isaac Denton. After speaking outside with Denton, one of the men shot him as he turned to go back inside the house. Denton died a few hours later but named W. B. Brockett and James Hardwick as his assailants. The same group of men next stopped at the home of Mr. Davis, also along the Little Osage. Mr. Davis refused to come outside after being called and a load of buckshot was fired through the door.[31] Next, the group went to the house of Mr. Hedrick. As he stepped to the door, he was shot with a shotgun and died immediately.[32]

Then, on the night of April 1 an old man named Travis, who was a friend of Hardwick, was brought before the Squatter's Court and tried for the murders. Finding Travis not guilty, the court released him. Travis rode to the home of the two Wasson brothers, where three of the men before whom Travis had just been tried had followed him, and after conversing with him for a short time one of them shot and killed Travis, and the other severely wounded the two Wassons.[33]

This new round of killing along the Little Osage caused settlers around Mapleton to organize a Protective Society and they chose James Montgomery as its leader.[34] Montgomery and his men now began ordering obnoxious families along the Osage to leave. After completing this along the Osage the men moved on to the Marmaton. They were thus engaged on April 21, when some of the men whom they had forced to leave made a requisition for a posse of United States troops, and a company of 20 men was sent out under Captain Anderson, along with the deputy marshal to arrest Montgomery and his men.[35]

In the following skirmish, the first and only time when free-state men fought with U.S. soldiers, one trooper was killed, several horses shot, and one free-state man wounded.[36] This event, known as the Battle of Paint Creek, caused a temporary stir of excitement and was applauded by the Lawrence *Republican*.[37] Leonhardt also described the battle and again gives new information not found elsewhere:

> In the middle of April we learned that the US troops would be withdrawn from fort scott & fearing that now Hamilton would likely come out & execute his plans. We made a Dash into each Prosalvery settlement where we expected to draw him out into an open fight. Montgomery and 16 men dashed first over the Marmaton River about 12 miles from fort scott but Hamilton fled into the fort, Judge Williams induced Capt. Anderson with a squad of US Soldiers to go and catch Montgomery. This brought on the fight on Yellow Paint Creek. We did fight Uncle Sam. Capt. Anderson was shot in the loin & his horse killed. His trooper on the right of him fell mortally wounded and several horses were also wounded. The orders were to kill rather the horses first but the men if forced to do so. Ben Hurley was the only one wounded on our side from troops on the Hill who had not come into the ravine. A flag of truce appeared asking us to promise to release their fallen commander & carry away the wounded. We granted this request. Capt. Anderson who had sworn to kill every ____ __ _____ was now pulled from under his fallen horse. He never troubled us any more, but resigned for fear of being court martialled [sic] for cowardly conduct in front of the enemy & for making war upon citizens. . . . We retired back into a circular thicket of close underbrush which the troops reinforced to over 200 did not dare to penetrate. We fired first & from that moment all fear of US troops had gloriously vanished.[38]

Leonhardt noted the names of a few men that were with Montgomery at Paint Creek, listing Eli Synder, Oliver Bain, Jennison, and the fighting preacher, John E. Stewart.[39]

Montgomery's tactics apparently worked, as an excerpt of a letter from Augustus Wattles to William Hutchinson dated April 28, 1858, attests:

> Nearly all the settlers had left the Little Osage. There is not a single inhabitant of Sprattsville left. I met at Moneka, freight wagons of movers with 30 yoke of oxen going north who left the vicinity of

Mapleton. They were free state men. They tell the most distressing tales. Today I have seen several proslavery families moving from the Marmaton & Little Osage. They tell tales equally harrowing. Property stolen or destroyed—families violently removed—men shot down in cold blood—and the whole country in anarchy & blood. no man obeys the laws & but few appeal to them.[40]

With most of the pro-slavery men now pushed out, Montgomery's objective had been completed. However, many of the men who left had gone only across the line into Missouri and were waiting for an opportunity to come back and exact revenge.[41]

On May 19, 1858, a group of approximately 25 men led by Charles Hamelton crossed into Kansas and carried out this threat. The group rounded up a large number of free-state men, let some go, then herded the 11 remaining men into a ravine near Trading Post and shot into them. Five men were killed and five wounded; one was unhurt. This event, known as the Marais des Cygne Massacre, shocked the people and created an uproar of agitation and rumors. Leonhardt wrote that the "events of May 19 brought many new recruits into Montgomery's camp,"[42] and Tomlinson (1858) recorded Montgomery's feelings:

> I did say in a moment of excitement, while standing over the dead bodies of the men killed at that terrible massacre . . . that for every dead man laying on the ground . . . I would require ten of his assassins, and for every wounded man I would have five, but in a short time that feeling passed away.[43]

How short a time that took is unknown. According to the *Missouri Republican,* May 28, 1858, Montgomery took action the next day:

LANE'S BANDITTI

> The Danite band organized by Lane, not content with stealing and murdering in the Territory of Kansas, have, it would seem, found its boundaries altogether too contracted for their thievish propensities, and they have pushed their adventure into Missouri. The following letter, from a well informed source in Jefferson City, presents a detailed account of the exploits of the banditti, in Bates and Cass counties. Of its entire correctness we have no doubt. . . .

Jefferson City, May 26, 1858.
Editor of Republican: Yesterday a special messenger arrived in this city bearing a statement signed by many of the most reliable citizens of Cass and Bates counties. . . . On the day subsequent, MONTGOMERY'S party supposed to number between two hundred and two hundred and fifty men . . . crossed the line into Missouri, and proceeded to Westpoint. . . . In the language of the statement, they "menanced, insulted and outraged the citizens of that place, who were in a defenseless condition, in the most shocking and brutal manner.". . .[44]

Shortly after this on June 7, Montgomery and his men set fire to the Western or McKay's Hotel in Fort Scott and reportedly shot at anyone who attempted to put it out, but the fire burned itself out.[45]

Governor Denver, accompanied by Charles Robinson and others, went south on an inspection tour on June 9 to see what could be done to relieve tensions in the area. At a large public meeting held in Fort Scott, proposals were laid out to restore peace in the area and although at one point the meeting almost turned into a riot, the result was a series of resolutions generally known as the Denver Peace Treaty.

The plan that was adopted on June 16, 1858, called for a withdrawal of troops from Fort Scott, an election of new officers in Bourbon County, the stationing of troops along the Missouri border, and suspension of the execution of old writs, and Montgomery and his men would abandon the field and go home.[46] The terms of the Denver Treaty were a compromise in that the free-state men agreed to abide by the decision of the court and to resort to law in the settlement of their disputes. However, the free-state men finally held control of the local government.[47]

Writing about the spring of 1858, Leonhardt later claimed that "among the most important and conspicuous deeds of the seceding Danites, I must mention the forcible [sic] retaking of such claims, from which free State settlers had been driven during the winter of '56 and the complete route [sic] of all obnoxious proslavery men, who harbored floating border ruffians."[48]

6

James Lane and His Danites

General James Lane, the former colonel who had distinguished himself in the Mexican War, first received military status in Kansas as a commander of the militia forces that defended Lawrence in 1855. Later, he was given the authority to raise a militia to protect the ballot boxes. At the mass convention at Grasshopper Falls in August, 1857, Leonhardt described a speech delivered by Lane, in which Lane asserted, "The Legislature belongs to the majority of the people, we have it, it belongs to us by right and gentlemen we are going to have it. By the ballot if we can, but by the bullet if we must."[1]

Although violence would continue in territorial Kansas until early 1859, events in October and December, 1857, and January, 1858, became the last pivotal episodes of the political contest in Kansas between pro-slavery and free-state forces. These events, including planned assassinations, led to a struggle which split the Free-State party and pitted General Lane against the more conservative faction in this party. Although Lane held on to the reins of power, this contest in the end strengthened his political enemies. The bottom line in this struggle was that the conservative side of the party favored a voting policy that would take part in the upcoming elections and attempt to elect free-state men to replace the pro-slavery legislature. The radical wing of the party favored a fighting policy to try and drive the pro-slavery men out by that method. Lane was opposed to taking any part in the October elections.

The election held on October 5, 1857, showed a free-state victory until returns came in from the small towns of Kickapoo and Oxford, as well as McGee County. These returns, of over 3,000 pro-slavery votes from communities that contained only a few hundred legal voters, threatened to tip the scales in favor of the pro-slavery forces. According to G. Brown, Governor Walker, who had pledged to oversee a fair election, decided to go ahead and certify the fraudulent votes. Only after a prolonged talk with Brown and the promise of help from Brown's *Herald of Freedom* did he agree not to count those votes.[2]

It was during this tense time, when it did appear Walker might go back on his word, that Lane proposed his first radical scheme. Augustus Wattles, an associate editor at the *Herald of Freedom* rushed into Brown's office:

> Why Brown, we are on the eve of a revolution! Gen. Lane has ordered the organized Free State forces of the Territory to assemble on Monday next, with arms and three days supply of provisions, the purpose of which is to march on Lecompton and kill every member of the Constitutional Convention. It is also his purpose to wipe out the Territorial Government, and set up the Topeka Government. The United States troops are *en route* for Utah, and now is thought a good time to strike. Unless headed off in his insane movement, notwithstanding our recent success at the polls, all is lost; for the country will never indorse [sic] this scheme of wholesale murder![3]

Brown wrote that he informed the more prominent men in Lawrence of this plot and a meeting was organized to learn the facts. Lane was brought in and questioned. He was evasive at first but became bolder as his supporters arrived and the feeling was it would not be a good time to vote on Lane's wild scheme, so the meeting was adjourned until evening.[4] At this meeting Joel K. Goodin arrived, took the rostrum, and related that:

> . . . he had received an order from his superior to report at Lawrence, armed and equipped for efficient military duty, and to bring provisions and camp-equipage for three days' service; that, "in obedience to that order, I am here to-night with my command, having made the journey all the way from Centropolis especially to obey it. [Cheers.] . . . We have worked all summer in a quiet way to regain the rights wrested from us by the invasion of the 30th of March, '55, and in spite of fraud and artifice we have triumphed. . . . But here is that Lecompton Constitutional Convention threatening us with new danger, when we supposed our dangers were all passed. Gen. Lane tells us that further peaceful measures are out of the question; that our only remedy for this new trouble is by shedding blood. I fully agree with him! [Boisterous cheers.] Nothing but blood will quiet this agitation, and restore tranquility to Kansas. Nothing but blood will make Kansas a Free State. [Cheers.] I came here expressly to spill blood, and I propose to do it before I return home. [Protracted

cheering.] It is not just that the whole country shall be convulsed; that disorder and violence shall be continued; that the perpetuity of the government shall be endangered by a revolution, when a little waste of worthless blood will restore order and tranquility again. [Cheers on cheers.] But I may differ with some of you as to the proper place to begin this blood-spilling business. [Hear! Hear!] No person has occasioned more strife, or been the more fruitful cause of our disturbances than—James H. Lane! He demands blood! We all want it; but it is his blood that is demanded at this time; and if he presses on his assassination project, I propose he shall be the first person to contribute in that direction." [The wildest cheering possible, greatly prolonged, followed.][5]

In the end, the assassination scheme was negated, a march was made on Lecompton to deliver resolutions protesting against the convention,[6] and Governor Walker decided not to certify the illegal votes. Leonhardt, though he wasn't yet officially in the Danites and was still back east on a speaking tour during that month, later wrote, "We Danites had Robert J. Walker, L. S. McClain [sic] and the whole outfit in LeCompton in charge for action at a moment's notice. Had Governor Robert J. Walker dared to permit those bogus Ellection [sic] returns to be officially counted against us he and every one of those prominent Conspirators in the Outrage would have been taken in the care of the silent workers of the Danites. That much I can disclose, their treacherous blood was never intended to stain our hands. . . ."[7]

Lane's ideas of assassination continued through the fall of 1857 as evidenced by a speech made by Lane and carried in the Leavenworth Kansas *Weekly Herald* in November, 1857. The following is an excerpt from that speech:

> . . . I have stood here on Kansas soil and seen a fraudulent Legislature forced upon us by a neighboring State. I have seen invasions come pouring in upon us. I have seen crime in every shape committed upon the settlers of Kansas, but this last act crowns them all in villany [sic] and fraud. And I speak here in Leavenworth responsible for all that I may say, that these villians who have committed this last great fraud, have forfeited their lives to an injured people. . . . I told a member of that Convention last night, that we will head them or behead them. I am not going to advise war or bloodshed here to-night, for perhaps there is no need of that. We have now got the goats so separated from the sheep that we can easily kill them without committing crime. For

Oliver P. Bayne
(Courtesy Rochelle Wright)

James Redpath
(Kansas State Historical Society)

Reverend John E. Stewart
(Kansas State Historical Society)

John Brown
(Kansas State Historical Society)

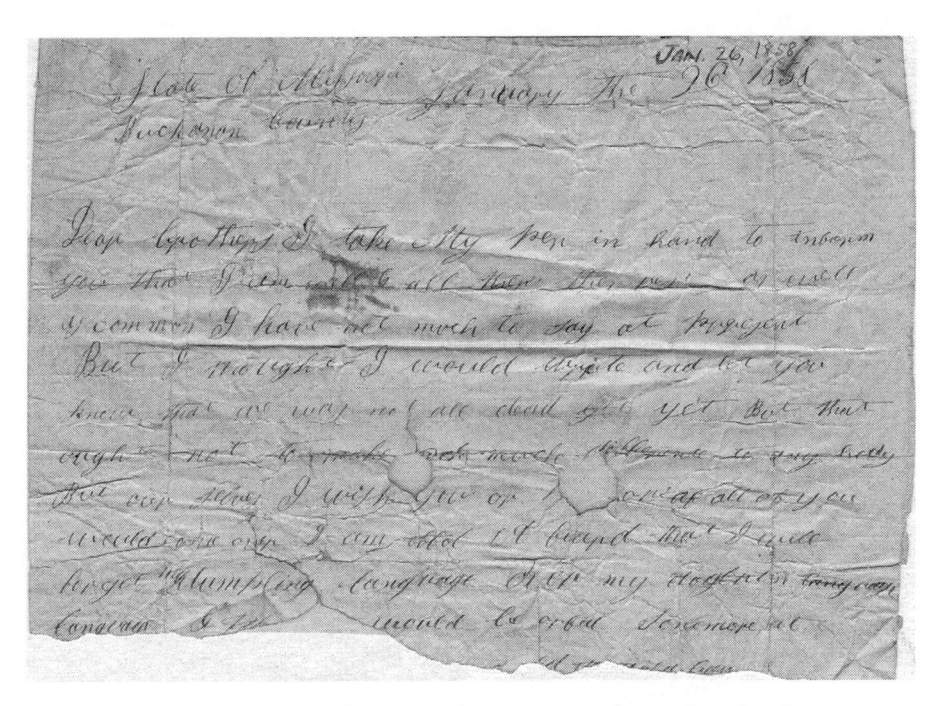

Danite message from "unknown member of Lodge in Buchanan Co. Mo." January 26, 1858.
(Kansas State Historical Society)

Richard Hinton
(Kansas State Historical Society)

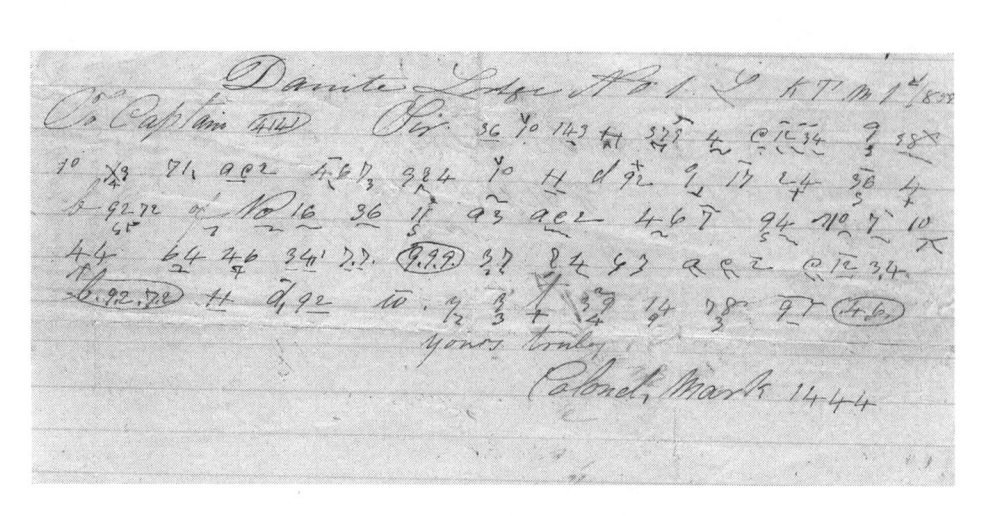

Danite secret cipher message dated May 1, 1858.
(Kansas State Historical Society)

James H. Lane
(Kansas State Historical Society)

Charles and Esther Leonhardt
(Kansas State Historical Society)

Leonhardt's grave at the Paola
Cemetary, reads C. W. Leonhott
(Author's Collection)

James Montgomery
(Kansas State Historical Society)

I truly believe if God should show his special Providence to-night we should see in these starry heavens his hand commanding us to exterminate those damned villians.... If I had my way though, I would send Jack Henderson and the rest of these scoundrels where they never would breathe pure air again.... These men who framed this constitution were the men who committed these outrages summer before last! They deserve death for those acts, and they deserve a thousand deaths for framing this constitution.... You may say, "Lane, you are excited." I say, ought we not be excited? Have we not suffered enough to excite every nerve in your body?... Should we not feel like taking these villians by the throat and choke their very life from them? I feel so. I cannot help it.... But I still believe there is no other safe way than by force. Take these men and give them a fair trial, but if you find them guilty of performing this fraud, they should suffer death....[8]

By late fall of 1857:

Having lost control of the territorial legislature the only hope of the pro-slavery party lay in admission of the state under the LeCompton constitution. In meeting the new crisis the free-state men were divided. The radicals, now organized into a secret society known as the "Danites," with Lane in command, urged aggression. The conservatives, led by G. W. Brown, S. N. Wood, P. C. Schuyler, and Thomas Ewing, Jr., favored nominating candidates under the LeCompton constitution, "that it might be speedily changed if admitted." The Lawrence convention of December 2 was reconvened on December 23 for a two-day session to decide upon a policy. By a "characteristic trick" the Lane men controlled the convention and it decided against participation in the election of January 4, 1858. The conservatives, however, led by G. W. Brown, bolted and assembled in the basement of the *Herald of Freedom* building, where a state ticket headed by G. W. Smith for governor and W. Y. Roberts for lieutenant governor was nominated. Although Lane "would have preferred to have pitched in he gave the ticket his reluctant support...."[9]

Mr. Stephenson, who wrote this passage in 1928, quoted heavily from other sources. Although correct in his summation of the politics, it appears Stephenson failed to take into account that the Danites had an earlier organization of December, 1855, even though he used James Legate's quote that the society had its birth because of the murder of Dow and Barber, which he should have known took place in November and December, 1855. He may have been confused, thinking that it was at this point, December, 1857, that Lane took over the Danite organization himself, even though it had been organized earlier. And as we shall see, even though Lane gave his "reluctant support" to the ticket, it was only superficial and he had other tricks to attempt.

Part of Lane's next trouble began on December 16, when the bill appointing him as major general and authorizing him to organize and regulate the militia was passed over the veto of Acting Governor Stanton.[10] This act and a similar one in 1858 "created a military board consisting of a major general, eight brigadier generals, and the usual complement of subordinate officials," but it also placed the board at odds with the governor, as he would "naturally refuse to recognize the military board, since he considered that the act that created it conflicted with his own position as commander in chief of the militia under the organic act. Out of this conflict of military authority there arose a bitter quarrel between Lane and Governor Denver,"[11] who replaced Stanton and officially assumed his duties on December 21, 1857.

Serious words and accusations were exchanged between Lane and Denver and a challenge was supposedly made by Denver to Lane. Accordingly, this is when the threats were made against Governor Denver's life. James Redpath, another free-state newspaper writer who, like Richard Hinton, decided not only to report the news but also to participate in it as well, turned against Lane. Redpath, an early arriver in territorial Kansas, had joined the Danites and later became a follower of John Brown. However, early in 1858, Redpath broke from Lane* and accused Lane of plotting to kill Governor Denver. Redpath also gave evidence that a secret Danite group existed in Kansas. The following is from the *Leavenworth Herald*, May 29, 1858:

> Redpath of the "Crusader of Freedom" is pitching into Lane and is making disclosures of a nature not altogether agreeable to him: Lane succeeded in enveiling [sic] Redpath into pecuniary liabilities, for the purpose of making a tool of him, in his schemes of assassination and robbery, but it appears that "the horse kicked out of the traces;" the account which Redpath gives of his connection and experience with

---

*According to Solomon Miller, Lane had seduced Redpath's wife. White Cloud, *Kansas Chief,* Oct. 27, 1864.

Jim Lane, and we believe it to be true, is sufficient to damn that man in the estimation of every honest man. . . . Jim Lane is now exposed by his own man Friday, as a fiend, embodying all the qualities of the liar, scoundrel, seducer and assassin . . . but the developments which Redpath makes, proves that not one half has been told concerning him; It will be recollected that the valiant General was particularly idigant [sic] that the Herald should republish an article from the Platte City Atlas, charging that a band of abolition Danites existed in this Territory and excited the people of this city to demonstrations of violence against us and our property. We stated at the time that it might be true; now we know and believe it to be true, and to sustain our belief we introduce Redpath as a witness—hear what he says: "On another occasion he told me—the request sounded like a command—to praise him for his magnanimity. [And] a few weeks before, he had tried to make me the agent for assassinating Robert S. Kelly—as he was then pursuing Mr. Shephard, with whom he quarralled [sic] when he could not make him a tool—with malignity which it would be euphony to characterize as infernal, I peremptorily refused to do so. Lane organized a club of Danites in Doniphan County. I became a member of it. Although he could have attended it, and was expected to attend it, he attempted, on the second night of its meeting to make me the agent to induce the Club to kill Robert Kelly [sic]. . . . I never hated Lane till he asked me to do this deed. I did indeed despise him from the bottom of my Soul, but I did not believe him to be capable of a scheme so diabolical—to involve a young man without any cause, in a criminal act of private revenge. It was so cowardly, contemptible and hellish that I left him without saying a word. . . . What do the conservative Free State men say to this? It has been denied repeatedly that any such organization as the "Danites" ever existed in the Territory, yet here we have direct proof that James Lane himself was at the head of such an organization and organized them merely to satisfy himself in his schemes of personal revenge by procuring the cowardly assassination of political enemies, whom he dared not face himself. . . . Had the expected difficulty between himself and Governor Denver been brought to an issue, we are furnished with the course he intended to pursue, by the developments of Redpath, who says: We are ready to swear in any court of justice or make solemn affidavit of the fact that Gen. Lane intimated to us that if Gov. Denver challenged him, he would have him put out of the way by the secret order known as the Danites.[12]

This must have coincided with the article referred to by Leonhardt when he wrote the following:

> L. McAthur of Topeka, late U. S. Disctrict Clerk in Lecompton and the same gentleman who signed those famous writs against free state men to be tried at the October term 1857 has this to say about Gov. Denver's knowleldge of getting killed by some of Lane's men, to wit—: Lane wrote a circular dennouncing [sic] Gov. Denver in most wild language, saying among other things: Denver would either challenge him or cowardlike, pay no attention to it. Well, Denver did pay no attention to Lane's Language. But we all were carefully watching things. Pretty soon afterwards Redpath fell out with Lane and he issued great big Handbills stating therin [sic] that had Gov. Denver actually challenged General Lane there would have been no Duel because Denver would have been killed secretly by the working Order of the Danites by the stern? Order of Lane. And Mr. L. McArthur still believes in Redpath. <u>And Now a little secret history</u>. Gov. Denver came very near being killed! Br. Coleman, Br. Macy and _____† now of Kanwaka Township, Douglas County, did go over to Lecompton for the sole & determined purpose to interview Gov. Denver to learn from his own mouth, his actually [sic] state of mind towards the pending issues between the parties & had voluntarily agreed among themselves, should they find Gov. Denver a foe to the free state movement they jointly would then & there kill him on the spot. Br. Coleman had agreed to drop his hat, as a sign to fire. But it turned out, that Gov. Denver talked very pleasantly & Coleman smiled to his Brother danites, saying: "Well gentlemen I think Gov. Denver is all right, let's be going home." The above is from Brother Coleman himself and many a laugh we both have had over this farce.[13]

As noted in chapter 2, one can speculate that, since Redpath had fallen out with Lane and exposed the Danite group in Doniphan County, as well as had given an account of the plot to kill Governor Denver, then it may also have been Redpath who leaked the text of the Danite secret oath to the *Leavenworth Herald* in July, 1858.

Nor are these revelations about a possible killing of Governor Denver the only ones that concerned assassinations. As noted before, Charles Robinson, the free-state leader in Lawrence who generally

---

†This name was left blank by Leonhardt, not because it was illegible.

advocated nonviolent methods, admitted in his own book (1892) that he had gone to one meeting and joined what he assumed were the Danites but then failed to attend after that. At the one meeting he attended, an assassination plot was discussed and became the reason he quit the group. Robinson related:

> Not long after the Military Board was organized Lane became thirsty for blood and proposed a general massacre of pro-slavery men. Robinson was in Lawrence at this time and he was invited to join a secret order, which he accepted. After the initiation ceremonies Lane arose with great dignity and said he had ordered General _____* to strike at Leavenworth, General _____* to strike at Atchinson, General _____* to strike at Kickapoo, and other places were to be struck by other generals, closing his solemn announcement by saying, "It now remains for Lawrence to say what shall be done with Lecompton." After this revelation, silence reigned for the space of several minutes, when from different parts of the room Robinson was called for. He responded to the call, and said he had heard a very remarkable statement and he would like to know by whose authority this general massacre was to be made. Lane replied, "By the authority of the Military Board." Robinson said that neither the Military nor any other board had any such authority, and he gave notice that whoever attempted to execute any such orders would have him to fight.[14]

What's important about this statement is Robinson's inclusion of the part about the Military Board. Since the board wasn't approved until December 16 this could not have been at the same time as Lane's scheme in October. Also, we have Robinson's statement in his book that at the time the convention was to meet in October he was "absent from Lawrence when this blow was to be struck," and "Lane took to the warpath and gathered his forces. . . ."[15] Thus, it would appear that the scheme to kill the legislators at Lecompton could not have been the same one when Robinson was initiated into the Danites, then told them he would have nothing to do with any plans of assassination.

George Brown related this same conversation with Robinson in Brown's book and about the plan he further stated:

> Whether this proposed general movement against the leading pro-slavery towns of the Territory, was planned to come off at the same time with the proposed military descent on Lecompton, we are not advised; but, from the date of an order in Gen. Lane's handwriting,

signed by him, and now in our possession, directed to "Capt. Charley Lenhart,"‡ ordering him to "take such a number of active young men as shall deem necessary, and proceed with as little delay as possible to colonize Kickapoo," we are convinced that the two periods were concurrent in time.[16]

At the next election, on January 4, 1858, more fraudulent votes were again made by Missourians, but the fraud was uncovered in an episode known as the candle-box affair. The story is told by Thomas Ewing, Jr.

The night before the election, Ewing had organized a company of about 30 free-state men. These men went to Kickapoo to observe the voting there. Just before the polls closed, Mr. Currier and Mr. Ewing voted. Their votes were numbered 550 and 551. Only two more votes were cast after that, totaling 553. Those election returns, along with all the rest, were sent to John Calhoun, the surveyor-general at Lecompton, which he certified showing the entire pro-slavery ticket elected. Calhoun then left for Washington to report the results.

Ewing, suspecting fraud, had the Territorial Legislature appoint a board to investigate the matter. The board called in L. A. McLean, Calhoun's chief clerk, to testify. McLean swore that Calhoun had taken all the returns with him to Washington. Later Ewing was told by an informant that the returns had instead been placed in a candle-box and hidden in a woodpile outside McLean's office.

Ewing obtained a search warrant and sent Sheriff Sam Walker to search the premises. Walker recovered the candle-box and returned it to the investigating committee. The returns showed that at Kickapoo after the polls closed at 553 voters, 442 additional names had been added as having voted. Additional names also swelled the returns from Oxford and Shawnee. At Delaware Crossing, the election judges' return had been spliced with a sheet of paper containing 336 additional names written in different handwriting and ink than the original. The addition of these fraudulent votes had given the pro-slavery ticket a victory, and Ewing swore out a warrant for the arrest of McLean.[17]

---

‡G. Brown's account reads Charley Lenhart. Charles Robinson's account reads Charley Leinhart. (Page 379, Robinson, *The Kansas Conflict*.)

Leonhardt himself admitted he and Reverend Stewart went on a mission, although not on Lane's orders, to eliminate McLean after the two of them had already seceded from Lane's Danite band, saying "that Captain Stewart was pledged to remain with myself members of the old—or Lane Ordre [sic], to see to matters needed our attention in LeCompton. Thus we both were send [sic] to take L. A. McLean on January 29, 1858."[18] In a different outline for his book, Leonhardt wrote, "After the candel [sic] box Calhoun affair, the writer had obeyed an ordre [sic] to take care of McClain [sic]. _____ _____ - Rev. John S. Stewart x x x"[19] No assassination took place, however, as McLean had wisely left the country as soon as the candle box containing the votes had been discovered.[20]

That Leonhardt knew much about Lane's wild assassination schemes is also evidenced by the following passage, while giving the modern reader another piece of knowledge about the connection between the Danites and Ohio City. Writing about local Kansas history, he noted:

> I consider Ohio City entirely gone out of existennce [sic] & now one of the many farms owned by the Hon. P. P. Elder of Ottawa. It was here where James H. Lane in Dec. 1857 on his way to the front saw fit & proper to sow a few bushels of whirlwind, which might have turned into a hurricane if it had been a good season for that kind of a political crop to mature well![21]

Leonhardt also mentioned that "Gov. Sam Medary had insulted Lane by addressing him merely Mister & then it was, where the seed sown at Ohio City was feared by us, who had the cause the means ready, Lane understandingly to raise the hurricane."[22]

Of the seven secret Danite letters that somehow survived, six are between commanders, one of which is entirely in a secret code, and the other is from a member that lived in Missouri.[23] Blackmar noted that all these dispatches were signed by officers who went by an assigned number except for one. "The only despatch [sic] signed by any one's real name being one from Lodge No. 4, under date of March 27, 1858, and addressed to '4141'" and signed by General James H. Lane. It reads as follows:

Sir: There is business of the greatest importance now transpiring here and I would like it much if you would come with the utmost dispatch and bring fifty men with you. You will go to the president of the association treasury and draw as much money as you think will pay the expense, but that will not be much, as you will be traveling through thickly settled places. Bring two pieces of artillery and the ammunition and baggage wagons.

Yours in has[t]e
Gen'l J. H. Lane[24]

Another of the secret letters, dated March 3, 1858, is also addressed to Capt. "4141" and reads:

Sir you are requested to report yourself at the head quarters of this lodge on the 18th instant as your presence is required in the case of Hunter for the murder of Dow we have him prisoner and would have put him to death but that he requested that you should come and see him he says that he has intelligence for you that he will not unfold to any other person he says it is of service to the party

Yours truly Major, Mark 00035[25]

As late as May, 1858, it is obvious Lane's Danites were still planning something big. A letter dated May 14 reads as follows:

Sir the proposition having passed both houses it is getting time for us to organize therefore it is recomended [sic] that you get all things in readiness for the coming election on the Lecompton Constitution remember to note down every mans name and the place of his residence who votes for that Constitution You are to organize your Company and have them drilled both to horse and foot tactics And when you want arms you can get them at the arsnel [sic] No 16 As I have sent a requisition for 300 rifles 300 Colts revolvers and 300 sabers to be delivered unto you and if that is not sufficient you can have more by making out a requisition for them.

Respectfully yours
Lieut. general
Mark 18.76.43[26]

The passage where the writer requests a list of every man who votes for the Lecompton Constitution and his place of residence suggests a chilling reason for the need of 300 rifles and 300 revolvers.

And only two weeks later, another Danite note to Capt. 4141, dated May 27, 1858 stated:

> Head quarters Kansas
>
> Sir you are hereby requested to take a minute description of your company the names _____ and ability and every relative thereto and immediately transmit the same to the undersigned as it is confidently expected that we will soon commence active operations you will strictly observe those orders.
>
> Colonel 23 63925[27]

Perhaps it was only the killing of Gaius Jenkins by Lane a week from the date of this note that stopped this planned operation.

Another illustration of the permeation of the Danites in early Kansas is found in Brown's (1902) work. In his attempt to substantiate the things he wrote as being true, Brown asked several prominent men to write letters testifying to different facts in his book. One such letter, written by Sam Walker, the sheriff who found the candle-box containing both the real and bogus votes, admitted that he had been a member of the Danites. Walker noted, "I was also a member of the secret organization which you mention, but I am glad to write, I *never favored the murdering policy*. I was always for open war, not secret assassination."[28]

And a further example of the depth of the Danite organization is given by Leonhardt as he sketched events for March, 1858:

> We went on the Verdigris & the Neosho River to reorganize our Danite order & got ready for Self-Defense. Upon our return we found that in April our men had attacked the Ruffians assembled at Watson's & killed a few and wounded more. State here that we had obtained valuable News from our secret agents who were members in different Missouri Lodges of every move against us. This is the explanation of our different moves & in different localities which bewildered our foes & startled former friends.[29]

Support for Leonhardt's assertion that the Danites did indeed, have secret agents in the Missouri secret groups, and that these agents relayed information to the Danites, is also found among the Danite dispatches in the Territorial Records. Among the messages is one from an "unknown member of Lodge in Buchanan Co. Mo," dated January 26, 1858:

State of Missouri
                    January 26, 1858
Buchanan County

Dear brothers I take My pen in hand to inform you that I am well & all the rest as well as common I have not much to say at present But I thought I would write and let you know that we was not all dead yet. But that ought not to make _____ much difference to any body But our selves I wish you or _____ of all of you would come over. I am offol [sic] __ feard [sic] that I will forget my dumpling language ___ or my doglatin language. . . .[30]

What this unknown writer meant by forgetting his "dumpling language" or "doglatin language" is anyone's guess, but one could suppose it might be his description of the Danite secret cipher (see photos of the two messages on pages 55 and 56).

7

John Brown and the Danites

On July 5, 1858, Montgomery disbanded his company of men and retired from the field of action.[1] Only a few weeks earlier, John Brown, now using the alias Shubel Morgan, had returned to Kansas. Brown traveled south from Lawrence, met Montgomery, and shortly thereafter, enrolled a new militia company and Montgomery joined it.[2] The purpose of this organization is not fully understood, but guards were posted along the border to question any suspicious persons entering the territory. One possible explanation appears to be that by his presence Brown hoped to restore confidence among the free-state people of the area and to guard against another incident like the Marais des Cygnes Massacre.[3]

But was John Brown in the Danites? That is a difficult question to answer. G. W. Brown (1902) obviously felt Brown was connected with the Danites. In his book, again looking at James Lane's proposal to wipe out the legislators at Lecompton, G. Brown wrote, "I have one of the most exciting chapters in Kansas history, . . . and which may partially explain John Brown's reasons for hovering on the borders of Kansas during this interval."[4] Although G. Brown doesn't quote them, Robinson (1892) included a series of letters written between Brown and Lane and Brown and Whitman, Lane's supposed second in command of the Danites. These letters, written between September and November, 1857, are mostly about guns and ammunition that Lane was trying to get Brown to deliver to him. Robinson makes the point that Lane sounded as urgent after the election as before, as if he may need the guns for the move against the legislature.[5] As noted earlier, G. Brown felt that the assassination scheme described by Robinson was to occur at the same time as the move against the legislature. Even if this is in error, we know G. Brown still felt that with the evidence they had seen at the time, it appeared:

> In this proposed assassination of all the members of this Constitutional Convention, we have the secret of old John Brown remaining so long at rest—from the 7th of August to the 2d of

November—with all the members of his clan, who were members of this secret organization, and familiar with its plans, hovering on the Kansas border, watching hourly for advices from Kansas, delaying for twelve days after the period fixed for striking the fatal blow; thence, with a single son, overland to Lawrence; a brief interview with Gen. E. B. Whitman, a high functionary and second in command in this secret organization; a short visit to Gov. Robinson, who frankly told him he was damaging the cause of Free Kansas by his predatory operations along the border, and then his return east, "disgusted with the Kansas leaders!"[6]

It certainly appears that as much as he was a loner, Brown obviously acted at times in concert with the Danites or would have acted with anyone as long as his goals of bloodshed, war, and national arousal on the slavery issue could be accomplished. In one outline, Leonhardt noted that:

John Brown & James Montgomery having had no confidence in Lane's honesty as a politician agreed upon me to watch Lane's movement as a fit _____ in the many Topeka State conventions & other mass meetings and if possible persuade him into the need of an immediate advance of all our forces in order to test his capacities as a Military Chieftain. We all three had only too soon discovered the politican paramount* in him with no spark of genuine enthusiasm for the slave. Upon their request I had joined the Danites in order to have open passage from camp to camp and if needed force my mind upon Lane. See Lane's report to the Legislature Housejournal [sic] 1858. P. 84–85. How well these two Chieftains had read Lane. Lane's report has some talk in it, but more humumh [sic]. State here my own experience to contradict & explain his report. Who is living to testify to my charges? Col. J. B. Abbott in De Soto, R. J. Hinton Sacramento California and Rev. Joe Coppock, Iowa. . . . Washington Buchanan somewhere in Arizona digging gold ___ Sidney Clark might know his adrys [sic].[7]

In this passage are some strange claims, indeed. First, it sounds as if John Brown and James Montgomery knew each other earlier than has been previously believed and that the two of them, along with

---

*Leonhardt first used the word demogogue but crossed it out and used the words politician paramount.

Leonhardt, had entered into an agreement to circumvent Lane, should he prove to be a dud. If Brown was involved in this plan it would appear he had, indeed, chosen to act with the Danites. We do know Montgomery felt strongly enough about Brown that he went back east to participate in a failed rescue plan of some of Brown's men.

After Brown's Harper's Ferry failure, a federal investigation occurred that tried to find out how deeply Brown's plans of treason went. Obviously a connection was attempted between Brown and the shadowy, secret group of the Danites. About this Leonhardt noted:

> Thus it happened that the mere politician and News hunter for Eastern papers or men of large trust from friends abroad knew actually nothing even of the existence of our Order. This was fully experienced in that indignation meeting held in Lawrence soon after the return of Gov. Chs. Robinson from the Harper's ferry investigation in which W. A. Phillips & James H. Lane became the Ringleader. Both these men hated Robinson and thought it fit occassion to shelf [sic] him for ever because of his testimony given at the investigation. It proved two points to the writer who at that critical time happened to be out of Kansas. 1. The majority of that Assembly knew nothing of our Order but in their individual spite against Chs. Robinson volunteered a negative proof which the erring crowd was only too eager to accept as facts proven and 2nd. Those Danites present among most of all Lane himself, assented to the demands of the people of Lawrence and joined in the cry Crucify him. While Robinson had said, There is a secret organization in existence, all the rest said: it's a Lie! Who lied??? Robinson stood exactly where he always stood, while minding his own business....[8]

In a different outline, Leonhardt wrote, "John Brown was not a member of our Lodge,"[9] which could be taken to mean he was a member of another Danite lodge or not at all. But whatever the case, obviously Brown agreed with what the Danites were doing. After his return to Kansas, Brown ventured south and constructed an earthen fort near Fort Bayne, (the cabin where the Squatter's Court met, see chapter 4).[10] Fort Bayne was obviously used as a staging area for some of the Danite activities. One piece of evidence in the Leonhardt Collection supporting this is a roster of the militia that was enrolled at Sugar Mound. Leonhardt wrote that he copied the roster from James Abbott's papers during a visit with him. On page 2 he noted:

> I also copied the following:
> No 10 Camp near Sugar Mound Dec. 24, 1857
> To the Commissary General Kansas Militia.
> Pay to C. B. Bayne Eighty Seven 75/100 Dollars
> for provisions furnished upon the order of the
> Office of the 1st Regiment K. M.
> R. Gilpatrick Commissary
> Jas B. Abbott Col.
> H. Q. Kansas Militia
> Dec. 17, 1857
> to Gen. A. W. Phillips[11]

Further support for the connection between Fort Bayne and the Danites is found in a letter from Judge Williams in Fort Scott to Governor Denver dated March 5, 1858:

> One thing is clear . . . in protecting Fort Scott . . . to stop these outrages 15 & 20 miles distant on the Osage, more troops will be necessary, part of which should be stationed at some commanding point on Osage, to act promptly, and break up the Rendesvous [sic] at Fort Bayne.[12]

It is also believed that John Brown had by this time "already made plans to perpetrate a mass rebellion among the slaves in the South." After Brown had hired a former English soldier named Hugh Forbes to train his men, Forbes had a falling out with Brown and had "threatened to expose his plans." Possibly this was a reason Brown came to Kansas at this time, to throw Forbes off the trail.[13]

The period of uneasy peace after Governor Denver's efforts lasted until October 30, 1858. On that night, according to accounts, Montgomery, Kagi, and others were in Mongomery's cabin when a group of men approached it, attempted to get Montgomery to come outside, then fired as Montgomery opened the door.[14] This attack led to a renewal of hostilities soon after, and Montgomery, in attempting to find out the facts in the grand jury investigation for his breaking the ballot box, used the term *jay-hawking*, the first time that the term appeared in newspapers.[15] Although the term had been in use for awhile before this, Leonhardt stated in an outline for his book that he wanted to show that "under Montgomery . . . the actually [sic] Danites [changed] into Defenders of Home & Emancipators of Slaves." It was at this time, "the rougher elements in this Order became notorious as Jayhawkers."[16]

One of the results of this renewed jayhawking was the arrest of two of Montgomery's men, Benjamin Rice and John Hudlow. Montgomery decided to raid Fort Scott and rescue them.

Leonhardt wrote that "the Fort Scott affair was prepared by all three with Capt. Brown's knowledge, but he different [sic] and took no part in it."[17] This agrees with Alpheus Tannar's account that John Brown, with four or five others, joined the attacking party and hoped to command the entire force. A vote taken among the men to choose a leader resulted in the election of Montgomery. After being rejected, Brown refused to join the expedition. Montgomery, believing his forces too small to effect the release of the two men, had already sent aides to Lawrence for help. On the night of December 15 the free-state groups collected at Fort Bayne on the Little Osage. The Lawrence contingent was under the leadership of S. N. Wood; those from Emporia under P. B. Plumb; and the Osawatomie men under S. S. Williams. To these forces were added about 30 men from the Little Osage and Sugar Mound commanded by Samuel Stevenson and James Montgomery, respectively. They proceeded to Fort Scott, where Montgomery divided his men into three groups. These groups guarded the homes of some of the best-known men in town, surrounded the Free-State Hotel where Rice and Hudlow were imprisoned, and stormed the hotel and freed Rice and Hudlow. John Little, the former deputy marshall, fired at the group of men watching his store, slightly injuring Ben Seaman, but was later shot dead while looking out the window above the door.[18] Leonhardt wrote, "Capt. Seaman was shot in the hand by Little's bullet. Who fired the fatal ball _____ and killed Little? Why Jesse Craig."[19] Leonhardt's account agrees with Tannar's write-up and Leonhardt added:

> On the night of the 15th December we went to release Brother Benjamin Rice with 68 men & old Betsy. Cold chilly ride through pitch darkness over snow & ice. We divided into 3 companies (1) to surround sheriff Hill's house (2) To surround the hotel Kagi (3) to go in & release Rice. The doors we kicked open except the one where Rice was in & that Elias Snyder burst open with a bed rail or gunstock. Rice was chained to the floor & soon among his friends again. . . . Was Capt. Brown with us? Ans. No! No! he went part of the way but remained on the little osage. Capt. Eli Snyder and his son Elias affidavits if needed. He had asked Montgomery what his plans were in regard to the prisoners taken from fort scott & how he expected to arrange the affair of the attack. Montgomery's reply was: He had no plans left such things

for the moment & to spring up to arrange. Capt. Brown thought such impulses very wrong and objected to go any farther with the expedition. He was in favor of <u>burning</u> the town affidavits of Elias Snyder to that effect if needed.[20]

It was not too long after this that Brown and his men were at Fort Bayne when a slave named Jim Daniels came to the fort and asked for help in effecting his escape and his family's. Brown decided to launch a raid to help these slaves and divided his men into two groups and assigned each to raid farms in Missouri and liberate slaves.

The result of this raid by Brown and his men was the liberating of 11 slaves, one, a woman who was pregnant. One of the owners, a man named David Cruise, resisted and was shot and killed. The party returned to Fort Bayne and hid the slaves in the timber. In the following days the slaves were taken to Moneka, Osawatomie, Lane and finally Greeley, where they were hidden in one or more cabins while pro-slavery search parties looked for the fugitives. While there, the pregnant slave woman gave birth, making the total number now 12.[21] It has been disputed just where these 12 slaves were secreted, either at Greeley or Garnett,[22] but in a newly discovered letter, Jessie Carson, granddaughter of Martin Carson, a settler who ran an Underground Railroad station at Berea, a town less than 2 miles northwest of Greeley, noted this about John Brown:

> At one time he kept thirty slaves in the valley where it was thickly settled with timber for a mo. The place would be described today as south of the Paradice Hill corner just under the bluffs, five miles east of Richmond. At one time he brought twelve slaves to my grandfathers home, three miles east of Richmond about midnight they were almost exhausted. They needed rest so much, my grandfather let them sleep and rest all the next day in his barn while he carried on a big butchering he had planned, and that night my father rode a horse and conducted them to the next station near Ottawa.[23]

Although in error on the number of slaves, Ms. Carson's statement lends support to the Greeley site as the location where the slaves were hidden for a month.

Leonhardt recorded a different version of Brown's raid into Missouri and wrote:

> About John Brown going into Missouri after these slaves. This is the fact in the case: a negro slave who had permission by his master to go into fort scott for the purpose of selling brooms which he made, found

enough news to tell him if could possibly see Capt. John brown & tell him his troubles he would help him to freedom. This slave either found the Captains camp or he must have met with Kagi. He told Kagi that he and his wife & children were to be sold next Tuesday and begged him to help him on his journey north. Kagi replied that Capt. Brown was absent but that he would ___ the captain & ___ ___ he could depend ___ their help. Kagi instructed that this slave to get his family & friends ready the evening before the sale they would certainly come & help him. When Capt. brown arrived in camp & was informed by Kagi of all the facts in this case he replied—"if these slaves are to be sold on Tuesday we had better go right off, for it will be harder to get them away the Day before or after the sale." They started therefore on Sunday. When Kagi met thesame [sic] slave, he found him unprepared & it took some time to make that slave understand the reason of their coming sooner then [sic] expected. But as he recognized Kagi again, he fully trusted him & his men. Brown's men ___ took all the white men on the place prisoner, ___ 2 yoke of cattle, hitched them to an old freight-waggon [sic] with cover & some horses ___ back pay for work ___ to their masters. They took these prisoners into Kansas to avoid troubles but released them when in ___ Territory. . . . They went to Rev. Samuel L. Adair who kept them in his back kitchen and ___ cattle & waggon [sic] on to friend Sam ___ near Stanton. There they hid the cattle in a out of the way feedlot & took two waggons to pieces & ___ each wheel & other part of the waggon. There cattle & waggon remained till Adair had notified Dr. Gillpatrick & Capt. Snyder of the facts in the case. These two found that little cabin on the prairy [sic] & took these slaves away from Adair & furnished their food, till Capt. Brown's return, who now took care of his family. Thus Kagi and not Capt. Brown was the real Emancipator in that historical affair.[24]

On the night after Brown's raid in December, another raid took place, reportedly by Eli Snyder. According to reports, Snyder and his men crossed into Missouri and sacked and burned the store of Jeremiah Jackson, allegedly the site where Charles Hamelton planned the raid that resulted in the Marais des Cygnes Massacre.[25] About this incident Leonhardt wrote, "The Jackson affair was Stewart's, Rev. John E. Stewart & his boys went over to Missouri in Dec. 1858 & burned the store of _____ Jackson shot him in the face." And in a different outline Leonhardt added that he "must correct the Snyder affair."[26] If true, not only does this show the inaccuracy of some of the newspaper reports but also sheds new light on the attack and the continued activity of Reverend Stewart.

After spending a month secreted away in the cabin near Greeley, Brown moved his liberated slaves on to Lawrence by January 24, 1859, and while there obtained a team of horses to replace his oxen.[27] After a layover of a couple of days, during which time Leonhardt claimed Brown came to see him at his room at the Whitney House,[28] Brown and his party left Lawrence on January 25 and from there traveled to Topeka and then on to Holton. After a brief encounter with a sheriff's posse at Straight Creek, otherwise known as the Battle of the Spurs, because the posse fled, the group moved out of Kansas Territory sometime in early February, 1859, on its way to Iowa.[29]

As Brown and his group were moving northward, preparing to leave Kansas for good, other efforts were underway by the legislature and Governor Sam Medary to restore peace again in southeast Kansas and, by February 17, had passed the Amnesty Act, which "granted a general amnesty . . . to extend to all political difficulties in the southern part of the territory."[30]

From that point on, peace generally held in Kansas until the Civil War brought renewed border fighting; however, sporadic events continued and, according to Leonhardt, were conducted by men with connections to the old Danites. An example of this was his comments while writing about slave hunters and "mansteelers" that would entice and help runaway slaves until a reward was offered; then these men would turn the fugitives in. Along this line he noted:

> An organization of such mansteelers [sic] brought the more rabid abolitionists into the harness. Hines [sic] was such a manstealer & followed it as a business, we hung him after having tried him by a court of 12 men in camp. This was Nov. 16, 1860. Had a paper with these words written "Hung by the people of Kas. for manstealing" was riding a horse with a rope fastened to a limb & the horse led from under him. This affair caused the hanging of two free state men Guthrie & Catlin as Horsethieves but really as abolitionists. . . . Whenever the Ruffians returned according to the Resolution adopted at Raysville "to stay away forever" our men became idignant [sic] at their appearance but mad if they did engage in their former outrages. They caught one Stephen Paddock hung him to a tree. "Hung as a returned Border Ruffian" was pinned to his head.[31]

In a different set of notes Leonhardt related, "Russell Hinds of Linn County, a Kidnapper, [was] tried and hung by a Vigilanns [sic] Committee (The Old Danites)."[32]

8

John Brown and Harper's Ferry

With things now quieted down in southeastern Kansas and John Brown gone from the territory for good, Leonhardt decided at some point in 1859 to move to Cincinnati, Ohio, to enter law school. Not content to settle down and attempt farming at the time, Leonhardt had already sold his original quarter section land claim near Emporia for $1,000 to George Kirkendall during September, 1858.[1] Whether his decision to enter law school at this time was influenced by what John Brown was planning is unknown, as well as why he chose to attend law school in Cincinnati. One possible explanation for Leonhardt's choice on location could have been that he was using his connection with James Lane as a way to open doors. Lane had visited with then Governor Salmon P. Chase in October, 1856,[2] and had spent time in Cincinnati in January, 1857,[3] while on his tour drumming up support for Kansas. It could well be more than a coincidence that Leonhardt ended up as a clerk in the law office of Salmon P. Chase and Ball.[4]

Charles set up residency in Ohio and obtained a notary public certificate. In 1859 it appears there was no residency requirement to qualify for this[5] so it is uncertain how long Leonhardt had been in Ohio. He was granted the certificate on October 15,[6] the day before John Brown launched his attack on Harper's Ferry.

His length of residency is of interest because on August 20, 1859, a letter was mailed from Cincinnati to U.S. Secretary of War John Floyd, which outlined in detail John Brown's plans to attack Harper's Ferry and begin a slave insurrection. In a book written in 1894 by Leonhardt's friend and fellow Danite, Richard Hinton, Hinton placed the leak about Brown's plans on Leonhardt's shoulders:

> Early in 1859 Leonhardt removed to Cincinati [sic] and entered as a student and clerk the office of Chase (Salmon P.) and Ball. During subsequent months Colonel Leonhardt received several notes from

Kagi, as he himself informed me shortly after the Harper's Ferry attack. Edmund Babb, an editorial writer on the Cincinnati *Gazette*, now dead I believe, had been in Kansas two or three times during the troubles that followed the arrival of Governor Geary. I recall his first arrival at Lawrence, Kansas, in December or January, 1856–1857; he was a close friend of Leonhardt. . . . Leonhardt a generous soul, was apt to trust those about him. He gave me distinctly to understand that he made a confidant of his editorial friend, after receiving early in August letters from both "Isaac Smith" (John Brown), and John Henri (Kagi) from Chambersburg, Pa., informing him that the "mines" were ready, and the "workmen" needed. These were the terms agreed upon between Kagi and myself, as well as to Leonhardt and the others. Almost immediately after confidence was given to Mr. Babb the following letter was sent to John B. Floyd."[7]

One problem with this accusation is that Hinton again implied Leonhardt was in Lawrence in December, 1856, or January, 1857, to meet Mr. Babb and, as I have shown, that is highly unlikely and counter to other evidence, not that Leonhardt and Babb couldn't have met at another time.

Other writers, however, have identified one of Brown's own men, Richard Realf, as the leak, or Hugh Forbes, the former English soldier who Brown had hired to drill his men.[8] Perhaps the best answer for who the mysterious letter writer was is a Quaker named Moses Varney, who lived in Springdale, Iowa, and learned of Brown's plan and told it to A. L. Smith. Mr. Smith and his cousin decided to each send a letter to Secretary of War Floyd from different localities. Their hope was that the guard at the armory would be strengthened and Brown would choose not to attack the place. The reason for the letter is that these men wanted to warn Floyd in order to spare lives on both sides.[9]

Whatever the case may be, the letter was ignored by Secretary of War Floyd. Brown launched his attack anywhere from 8 to 10 days early, possibly because Brown suspected a traitor among his group.[10]

The initial attack on the arsenal was successful, but Brown continued to linger and ignored warnings by his men that they needed to leave. In the end, after the local men had prevented Brown from escaping, federal troops under the command of Robert E. Lee were called out and stormed the engine house where Brown and his men were barricaded. Brown lost 10 men killed during the raid and 7 more would be hung later, including himself.

Leonhardt, who was supposed to participate, wrote that he got there too late, and by the time he arrived there was nothing that could be done, "only a few burning haystacks told to the few remaining friends of this remarkable man, that his friends, though near, had become helpless to snatch from him his long anticipated and highly cherished crown of a martyr in his own chosen course!"[11]

One unidentified newspaper account in the family's possession said Leonhardt escaped Harper's Ferry with Coppic[12] [sic] and the obituary of Leonhardt in 1884 stated that he had been arrested in Philadelphia "under suspicion of being one of Brown's men but it could not be proven and he was released."[13] Neither of these claims can be substantiated. That Leonhardt knew of the plans ahead of time and planned to be there is corroborated by Richard Hinton's passage, "It is certain that he [Leonhardt] agreed to serve and was entrusted with the plan and intended movement."[14] However, Hinton goes on to say Leonhardt did not show up at Harper's Ferry because Edmund Babb "labored with the law student not to go further in the John Brown movement."[15]

I believe it is hard for modern readers to appreciate the danger and stigma associated with being implicated in Brown's plans; seven people were executed for treason, and public outrage and a congressional hearing were reason enough for Leonhardt to keep his involvement secret so long. What follows is Leonhardt's own written account of his involvement in the Harper's Ferry raid:

> Another very important question has often been asked of me to explain, but whose direct and full answer I had good cause to delay—my personal connection with John Brown and the Harper's Ferry failure. As all former fears are now entirely removed to hold the Republican party at large and its Leader responsible for it, I am willing to go on reccord [sic] with those few hot-headed abolitionists who knew well what they were about in that stupendous undertaking. Just before leaving for Canada to make preliminary arrangements for the future events in Harper's ferry John Brown and his ever trusty friend Kagi called on me at the Whitney House in Lawrence. E. D. Ladd, now deceased was then my roommate in No. #9. In that room it was were [sic] John Brown laid all of his Harper's ferry plans before me. Many storms have since that event passed over my head, but I freely confess, that it is utterly impossible for me to forget the deep impression John Brown made then upon me. In vain did I look back into my eventful past life. I had seen and conversed with some of the greatest Agitators

in my native country, but there were none who ever compared with him. In our Homestruggles [sic] during 1847 to 1849 we had often held our own life in our hands to be lifted upon the common altar as a blood offering for our country's sake as here this man pleaded the cause of another people and race, This counsil [sic] of conspirancy lasted for several days. My military training in Europe availeth me nothing with this civilian warrior. The praying fighter would calmly explain—"what of their vast numbers, let them come on, the host of Israel is on our side," His local knowledge of the topographical geography near Harper's ferry and all along the river was complete. He was well supplied with maps. I impressed than [sic] upon his mind the necessity of cutting the telegraph wire and destroying the bridge as soon as the arms had been obtained and then make for the mountains if possible the blue ridge, his first rallying point. I had my doubts of the Negroes rushing to him for arms. His reply was that matter has been attended to." I then repeated to him European failures to handle well the headless mob and proved to him this would be a more cruel one more so than we ever heard of. Two distinct races would thus take each other by the throat. The more intense the martyr got on that matter, the more military point of his extreem [sic] weakenss [sic] I proved. At last he responded: We don't cross a bridge till we come to it. Men from Canada were promised to take a leading hand to arm the slaves. All seemed plausible so far. His first plan was only to arm the slaves and look to the almighty to furnish the Moses to lead them into the promised land. To my question, but who among us is capable of handling this great mass of Negroes Insurgents he gave me no immediate reply, but walked calmly up to me, put both arms upon my shoulders and looking deeply into my eyes said: "you are chosen." He sat down to our washstand and penned in his clear letters verbatim as follows: John Brown. When I write that I would like to see you, interpret I am in earnest. When we parted, it was, to meet no more on earth. I received a facsimile of that same note, but too late for action. All was over already! only a few burning haystacks told to the few remaining friends of this remarkable man, that his friends, though near, had become helpless to snatch from him his long anticipated and highly cherished crown of a martyr in his own chosen course! But, who can tell, what might have otherwise happened, had his men from Canada, New York, & Boston been permitted to arrive in time to cooperate. It may perhaps not come amiss to state, that John Brown struck the blow a few days sooner than anticipated by us. What moved him to do so can only be surmised [sic] by what happened afterwards—the confession of John E. Cook.... Every writer, who either lauded, applauded, or besmeared the memory of John Brown, has seen proper to speak of a certain resistless power of mind and will, which this remarkable man exercised over those who came in contact with him. My own experience is a little at variance with that power. I highly admired, perhaps even loved the old man for his daring to do, what he considered his assigned duty. To pray unceasingly and fight against slavery most unsparingly. But still we both different [sic] vastly in the mode of striking at Billy Patterson and his many Allies. I am neither of puritanical stock, nor in the least connected with anybody whose forefathers landed at Plymouth Rock. As an American by choice, I am my own Ancestor. But as such, I could not withstand the proferred [sic] opportunity of critizising [sic] this puritanical fighter with the observing eye of the European exile. He could reconsile [sic] wars with christianity. I still fail to see these points. The Lord may respond to the fervent prayers of fighting men but I have scripture to prove that he sends leaness [sic] into their souls likewise. (see CVI 106 Psalm v. 15) while talking with the captain on this very topic he forced me to a severe task to defend my position and I related to him the recorded prayer of the prussian general, the Duke of Desson, known as the old Dessanir, while at the moment of charging against the Austrian Army. His prayer ran in this way and is an historical fact. Lord thou knowest best I don't trouble thee often with supplication for my men, nor myself at such times like these, but good Lord, if thou does not feel inclined to help us, do I humbly beseech thee let the Austrians also alone and than [sic] shall see how well I can lick them myself! This was rather a stunner. Laughingly he asked: and who got licked? Well sir, history has it the Austrians did![16]

Referring possibly to the school of thought that he somehow was involved in leaking John Brown's plans of attacking Harper's Ferry, Leonhardt stated:

I have no recollection that Brown ever unfolded his plans to newspaper correspondents, but remember distinctly his private opinion of all such, except Plumb, whom he held in fighting esteem. I know of three Quaker families in Iowa (station keepers of the underground railroad) with whom Brown and his men always found a home, who were cognizant of his Harper's Ferry plans. John E. Cook confided these facts to my mother-in-law and to James Townsend's family, Stevens or C.P. Tidd, to the family of Moses Varney. When Brown was about to leave and the last farewell about to be said to the members of my father-in-law's family, Father Griffeth Lewis felt it his Christian duty to plead with him alone, not to throw away his life. Both old gentlemen were deeply moved; but Brown's answer was, "I deem it my duty to do so for the poor, oppressed slave."[17]

9

Danites Reunited

Leonhardt graduated from the Cincinnati School of Law on April 15, 1860[1] and returned to Kansas in early June. According to his obituary, he attended the Republican National Convention in Chicago that nominated Abraham Lincoln for president.[2] The convention took place on May 16–18, 1860, so it is possible that Leonhardt attended while on his way from Cincinnati back to Lawrence. Leonhardt never stated in his writings that he actually attended the convention but noted:

> as the loss of healthy Rest undermines the body even of a Giant, and caused fearful waste and corruption in all of its vital tissues, even so in the body politic, when unsound elements are introduced. Such was the case with that fourth Resolution of the Chicago Platform, upon which Abram Lincoln was nominated "People do you remember that resolution?" "Slavery shall remain where it exists.—" It was the "basest political farce on record." Neither the framers themselves, nor the South could believe its fullfillment. Hardly had the ink become dry upon the paper, that produced this platform when we found the wildest excitement agitating throughout the border Slave States and the whole South for the first time in the great Anti-Slavery Tumult the fierce fireeater [sic] of the sunny South and the rabid Abolitionist of the North, joined issue. . . .[3]

Once back in Lawrence, Leonhardt ended up at "fort Stewart," the residence and Underground Railroad headquarters of his old partner in southeast Kansas, the Reverend John Stewart. There, an Underground Railroad trip was organized with Stewart, Leonhardt, and nine other men, several of whom were former Danites, including Warren Bassett and Joe Coppock. Washington Buchanan, the Danite whose playful prayer Leonhardt related, was the man chosen to remain behind at "fort Stewart" and protect Stewart's wife and children.[4]

This trip left Lawrence on June 13, 1860, and transported at least 13 escaped slaves from Lawrence, Kansas, through Nebraska into Iowa, to the Quaker communities of Springdale and West Branch, the same place John Brown had reached on his Underground Railroad trip and where he had recruited and trained for his attack. The trip was similar to Brown's in that there was a large group of slaves who were hidden in wagons. Leonhardt noted things had changed from earlier Underground Railroad (UGRR) methods in Lawrence. Before this time, the runaway slave:

> would be hid [sic] away and perhaps send [sic] over to Topeka in a day or two had hardly ever more than two or three men known of this fact. But now fugitives were constantly coming from all quarters and as if by some premeditated plan everybody abroad thought Lawrence a fit place to dispatch them to. For some time the old honored way of conveyance by night in a farm wagon to the next best farm whose sympathy was with us, did very well. But when Arkansas had passed the Law expelling all her free colored people or suffer enslavement a complete stampede took soon place, and we felt the need of some other way to dispatch them North.[5]

The fact that Reverend Stewart had taken over in Kansas where John Brown had left off is evidenced by the following extract from an article published by Joe Coppock in 1895:

> John Brown's raid into Missouri from Southern Kansas started an exodus from that region so formidable that slaves sold from one-half to two-thirds their former price. Not long after this the Fighting Preacher, Captain Stewart, under whom the writer was initiated into the mysteries of border warfare, did in Northern Kansas what Brown had done in Southern Kansas, and every slave was cleared out of the territory.[6]

Despite its obvious overstatement, the passage shows what Stewart was involved in after southeast Kansas settled down and that he had taken over the mantle of liberator after Brown left Kansas.

The Underground Railroad caravan, one that Leonhardt called "The Last Train," reached Springdale, Iowa, safely on August 17, 1860, and delivered the escaped slaves into the safety of the Quaker community.[7] While resting in Springdale after the trip, Leonhardt met and fell in love with the eldest daughter of an Underground Railroad station master named Griffith Lewis. Her name was Esther and the two found that "mutual sympathies ripened into mutual love."[8] Leonhardt remained with Esther's family in Iowa and opened a law practice. The two were married on April 18, 1861, six days after the firing on Fort Sumter and the beginning of the Civil War.[9]

Although Leonhardt did not return to Kansas for 10 years, he later claimed that sporadic, anti-slavery events continued to happen there. In August, 1861, Leonhardt decided to join the Union Army and traveled east to join the 58th regiment of New York volunteers.[10] Why he chose to join a New York regiment is unknown, but later in his life, as he was engaged in his writings and the work brought back memories, he mused:

> With this somewhat lengthy _____ of General James H. Lane I must confess my ardent wish & longing to have been permitted to pertake [sic] of the glorious results Kansas Regiments have achieved during the late war. Though myself in the Army my duties had fallen Among the Army of the Potomac. I sadly missed my former Kansas Coworkers _____ unison of whom I dearly desired to finish that work we had in Kansas so fearlessly commenced.[11]

After serving only a few months, Leonhardt was promoted to lieutenant and made adjutant. He was transferred to Virginia but caught a bad case of dysentery or ague and became very sick. He continued to suffer the effects and was mustered out of the army on January 2, 1862.[12]

Leonhardt returned to Iowa and continued trying to make a living as a lawyer but was never very successful.

In 1870, he returned to Kansas with his wife and five children and settled on a farm in Louisville, Kansas. There he was the police judge and attempted to do some farming. He wrote that, after his return to Kansas in 1870, men that he was involved with in the old days urged him to begin writing down some of the history from '57 and '58 so it would not be lost.[13] He began this task as early as 1873 and continued working on different manuscripts and giving lectures in different parts of eastern Kansas until 1882.

Leonhardt eventually came up with a complete manuscript that was ready for publishing, as evidenced by the following quote from an unknown newspaper clipping:

> During the past few years the general has been engaged in collecting material for a history of Kansas. . . . His work in now reduced to manuscript, which we have been permitted to peruse. It is entitled, "Stray

Leaves Belonging to the Unwritten History of Kansas." We unhesitatingly pronounce his work the most novel, entertaining, interesting, original and thrilling that has ever been written about Kansas. He has entered a field heretofore entirely unexplored by Kansas historians. He takes up Kansas militant history from 1857 and follows it up until the state became a member of the union. A full history and exposition of the doings of the Danites; the operations of the underground railroad; the details of the war in Linn and Bourbon counties in 1858; the deeds of John Brown and Montgomery and their men; are here given in faithful and vivid colors.[14]

Not able to find a publisher, Leonhardt tried to raise money and publish the book himself but this was also unsuccessful. Leonhardt also got back in touch with Richard Hinton. In a letter to Hinton in 1880 he addressed it "Brother Danite" and told Hinton he was still financially poor and his poverty was the reason he could not pursue trying to track down Reverend Stewart in Colorado as he dearly wanted to get his valuable contributions to his work.[15]

As his health continued to worsen, possibly connected to lingering effects from his Civil War illness, the family moved to Paola, Kansas, in 1881, where he was "in poor health and unable to perform any kind of manual labor . . ."[16] Leonhardt seemed to find some last strength and purpose helping put together an old settlers' reunion that took place at Lincoln Park in Lane, Kansas, on July 4, 1882. It appears that some of his last writing and efforts were spent on this project.[17]

For the reunion, a special train was scheduled to bring in folks from all around. According to the Lane *Advance* over 2,000 people attended, with the honorable P. P. Elder chosen as president of the day. "At 1:30 the people again re-assembled together for the purpose of organizing an Old Settler's Re-Union and elected officers. Then came the Old Settlers experience meeting which was replete with thrilling events, and hair-breadth escapes, too numerous for us to ever begin to think of narrating. Johnson Clark, J. O. Reese, Wm. H. Ambrose, H. Shively, Judge Roberts, H. B. Smith, Mitchell Barker, Joshua Baker, and last, but not least, in experience came Hon. C. W. Leonhardt."[18] It is also possible a manuscript he wrote and titled "Farewell to My Comrades," was a speech he planned to give, or did give, at this reunion.

Leonhardt was ambitious in the planning of this reunion and wrote:

> It is our united endeavor to bring the surviving members of the historic Squatter's Court together to hold its next session in Lincoln Park. We understand it will be a special term for the specific purpose of trying the Osawatomie Spy for contempt of History. Knowing something of the former _____ ruling in that august court, fears are entertained already, that _____ said Defendent [sic] will after refusing to plead & or be sworn upon x kiss the only books used in that Court, to wit—Dr. Gunns Works of God, man & the Devil, Defendent may yet receive the cruel sentence—to read aloud to us old Timers.[19]

According to a partial diary kept by Leonhardt during the summer of 1882, while working on the reunion, he became acquainted with several prominent men at Lane, including John Hanway, the son of the late Judge Hanway, who had been connected with John Brown. He also hooked up with T. J. Crowder, and Leonhardt was hired to write several articles. It also appears there were ambitious plans in 1882 to charter and open a John Brown Industrial School at Lane, Kansas, for both female and male black youth.[20] What happened to this proposed industrial school is unknown. As Leonhardt's health continued to fail he must have had to abandon his work on helping this group.

Leonhardt's health continued to worsen and he became bed ridden. As he grew weaker he was attended to by an old Civil War comrade until Leonhardt's death on September 7, 1884.[21] He was buried with military honors in the soldier's plot at the Paola Cemetery but his tombstone reads "C. W. Leonhott." The entry in the city clerk's book for recording deaths is also misspelled and reads "Charles Leonhott" but has his correct birthdate and place of birth.[22]

After his death, his wife, Esther, continued efforts to have his manuscript published,[23] but was not successful. Esther died on April 22, 1892, and was buried in Manhattan, Kansas.

10

Charles Leonhardt/ Charles Lenhart

It would be remiss to write a book involving Charles Leonhardt without mentioning another man equally involved in Bleeding Kansas on the free-state side—Charles Lenhart. That two men, Charles Leonhardt and Charles Lenhart, with almost the same name, would end up in Kansas fighting for the same side is a coincidence, but what is stranger is that they were both well known by General Lane, John Brown, Richard Hinton, and Reverend Stewart. Both were Danites, although Leonhardt in all his writings does not mention Lenhart, and both were at one time or another accused of leading the largest massacre to have taken place in Kansas history.

The confusion between these two men is understandable; a large percentage of the early settlers in Kansas did not read or write very well, and those who could frequently misspelled names. As previously mentioned in chapter 3, a write-up on the 1857 legislative session in which Leonhardt participated has his name spelled wrong four different ways—including Lenhart.[1]

That Leonhardt knew, or at least knew about, Lenhart is certain and evidenced by the articles which appeared in the *Old Colony Memorial* and *Plymouth Rock* in April and May, 1858. This is the story that appeared:

> Capt. Leonhardt Shot—Capt. Leonhardt, who has figured somewhat in the disturbance in Kansas, was shot Thursday night, the 18th inst. at Geary City. The St. Joseph Journal gives the following account of the affair.
>
> There was a ball at Geary City, and Charles Leonhardt, accompanied by a friend, entered the room with the avowed determination of "breaking up the ball." He commenced operations by firing a pistol ball through the ceilings which narrowly missed a young lady in the room above. He then fired another ball through a window, but

finding that pistol shooting did not disturb the equanimity of the Kansas beaus and belles, he retired doubtless in disgust. "The next scene of his exploits was Porter's grocery. After putting a hole through Mrs. Porters' [sic] Stove pipe, by way of introducing himself, he walked up to a card table where several persons were engaged playing and unceremoniously swept off all the "documents" [sic]. At a slight remonstrance from the clerk, he slapped that gentleman in the face with a bundle of wrapping paper. The clerk immediately drew a revolver and shot him twice, both balls taking effect in his right arm and side, and then seized a shot gun, which he was prevented from firing by the interference of parties standing by. Leonhardt, who was at this time in the doorway, again commenced firing and succeeded in slightly wounding his antagonist. "Leonhardt was taken to the printing office, where he lay in a critical condition. All the parties were Free State men, with the single exception of the friend who first entered the ball-room with Leonhardt."[2]

Next, the *Plymouth Rock* picked up the story and ran its own line:

Captain Leonhardt Shot—Under this caption the papers are giving accounts of a man, who formerly figured among the shallow pated simpletons hereabouts, that show him to have been either very drunk or very simple. The affair happened in Kansas, and we have no doubt the Jim Lane's and their associates will continue to bleed on, as though the "Cap'n" had neither shot a stove funnel nor been shot himself.[3]

In May, the *Plymouth Rock* ran this correction:

Charles F. W. Leonhardt. It is now said the reports which have been so extensively circulated derogatory to the character of this individual, who for some time resided in this town, and who is now in Kansas, are totally untrue, but on the contrary, Mr. Leonhardt occupies a very respectable position in society in Kansas. The individual to whom these unfavorable reports do apply, is one Charles Lenhart, who went from some of the Middle States.[4]

The Lawrence press also picked up the story and published this on April 29, 1858:

We notice in a number of our Eastern exchanges a statement that "Charles Leonhardt, a prominent German citizen in Kansas, was killed in a shooting affair at Geary City, when drunk." A mistake has been made by confounding our German fellow citizen, Col. C. F. W. Leonhardt, of Lawrence, with Charlie Lenhart, of Doniphan. The former gentleman has not been shot—has not been in a row—has not been drunk—but is now, and has been, quietly attending to his pursuits in this city. Charlie Lenhart *was* shot at Geary City, but, we understand, is nearly well again.[5]

Upon being made aware of the mistake, the real Leonhardt was genuinely hurt that people back in Plymouth actually believed he could be shot in a drunken row. In fact, although not the main reason he went back east in October, 1857, it appears Leonhardt could not resist stopping in at Plymouth on his speaking tour and letting the folks know how shocked he was they had believed the earlier story. The following is an excerpt from a long article he wrote during the summer of 1857, but it is one that he obviously planned to deliver at Plymouth:

> It is hardly one year since an unknown stranger pretending to come from Kanzas, on his way East, called at the house of one of your own citizens. he delivered there faithfully his mefsage, [sic] handed to him by one, to pofsess [sic] whose friendship remains an honor.
>
> Your humble servant was that stranger. One year sent its everlasting waves into the Ocean of Eternity, since we met, but alas! what a change has taken place. I see by the glance of many well known friendly smiles that you recognize the former stranger to-night as a welcome friend, who is coming back from a far journey. . . .
>
> But, as I have been informed to my great sorrow, that a few not far from this place residing, did not feel pleased in seeing a "foreigner" so highly honored, because in their political opinion they might have seen in me a dangerous foe to their already broken party. . . . Before proceeding further, I am under the necefsity [sic] to state to you, who had from the moment we met taken one to your homes and firesides, that gratitude to you as well as self respect compelled me to visit this place again in order to "face" those who jeeringly sneered at you when a false and malicious statement appeared in print, to the effect that I was <u>shot</u>, yes! shot and killed! and that too "in a drunken row." What a slander! what an insult! Could you who were thus designingly deceived not wait a moment to inquire into and ascertain the facts? . . .
>
> My Friends: if you should lose your humble speaker on the frontier of Liberty out on the far western border of civilization it will be in such a manner and such a spot only that I can appear before the

pure eye of Eternity as a <u>Man</u> who knew he was made after the Divine Image. . . . My Friends, if i have to go sudden, unprepared, it will be fulfilling duties Providence saw fit to bestow, and wearing, shall I not say it, the crown as a Martyr of Liberty. . . .[6]

The confusion between the identities of these two men would continue well after both were dead. Leonhardt gave us much information about himself, but it is much harder to find facts about Charles Lenhart. Lenhart was born in Iowa around 1836. He came to Kansas early in the territorial period during 1855, was hired as a printer by George W. Brown, and worked at the *Herald of Freedom*. He slept outside on the prairie until, months later, during a rainstorm, he asked Brown for permission to sleep in the printing office.[7]

The excitement surrounding the Wakarusa War and later the sacking of Lawrence, when the *Herald of Freedom* was ransacked and the printing press broken, seemed to have changed Charley Lenhart. Lenhart's employer, George W. Brown, explained:

> Charley did faithful service for Kansas during the Wakarusa war, in the fall of '55, but from that forth I could not count on him with certainty. If there was any wild adventure on foot he was the leader and away! After the destruction of the *Herald of Freedom* office in '56, Lenhart seemed to have adopted a guerilla life, and I only heard of him through others thereafter. He appeared intimate with both Lane and Brown, and held himself ever ready to execute their wishes. His associates were of the dare-devil stripe, of which John E. Cook was a representative. He was fearless and brave and always in sympathy with the *fighting* Free State men. . . .[8]

Lenhart was named as the man who shot Sheriff Jones in Lt. McIntosh's tent at Lawrence, and it appears Jones himself still believed that story later in his life, as implied from a conversation he had with Col. William Phillips in 1879.[9]

Accounts relate that Lenhart was "one of the first to take to the brush,"[10] after the sack of Lawrence on May 21, 1856, helping the free-state forces resist the advantage the pro-slavery forces had gained. A few days later, Lenhart, with a large group of other men, showed up after the Battle of BlackJack and helped John Brown's exhausted men guard the prisoners[11] Brown had captured until U.S. troops showed up and made Brown turn the prisoners loose.

Later that summer, Lenhart and his guerilla band set up camp atop the timbered ridges of Blue Mound* south of the Wakarusa River outside of Lawrence. Robert DeWitt, who published a pamphlet entitled "The Life, Trial and Execution of John Brown," had this to say about Lenhart's camp:

> Charley was encamped at Blue Mound—a wooded eminence south of the Wakarusa, and twelve miles from Lawrence. Near the summit of the Mound, in the thickest part of the wood, I found the young guerilla boys lying at their ease. Their horses were tethered at different places in the vicinity of the camp. The only covering they had was an old canvas (which they had taken from the enemy), and which, tied to trees, afforded a protection against the rain. Each man had blanket, rifle, pistol, and bowie-knife. The side-arms were stuck in their belts. Their browned faces and wild, rugged appearance, I thought, were unanswerable proofs of an "irresistible conflict."[12]

Writing about John E. Cook, Lenhart's close companion who was later hung for his part in the Harper's Ferry raid, DeWitt noted the following incident:

> Cook had an exciting and rough time in Kansas. He found a friend in Charles Lenhart, the organizer of the Free State guerillas, and with that party he had his first fight. On this occasion, among three or four boys who accompanied Cook, was a young gentleman named Stewart, the only son of a wealthy family in the state of New York. Charley Lenhart was chosen captain. They had not proceeded more than four miles, when they suddenly came upon three Missourians on horseback, who, as soon as they saw the Lawrence boys, drew up their rifles and fired a volley at them. Stewart fell a corpse—shot through the forehead. The rifles of the survivors were instantly raised; but, in consequence of the bad *pellets* which Sharpe's manufacturing company at that time made, they would not go off until several of them had snapped. By that time the Missourians, favored by the nature of the ground, were almost out of range. Only one of them was wounded. He was lying along his horse at the time, and the ball glanced along his back, taking a ribbon out of his coat from the waist to the neck. The wound, therefore, was trifling only.

---

*Blue Mound is a large, wooded hill southeast of Lawrence, still known by this name today.

Charley looked after them sternly; and then turning to his boys, he told them to kneel over the corpse.

"Hold up your hands!" he said, "and take this oath!"

I will not repeat that oath; suffice it to say that it was a terrible one, and kept. Stewart was revenged.[13]

The story of the alleged massacre—which both Leonhardt and Lenhart have been named as leading—relates that the pro-slavery group John Brown defeated at BlackJack, the Kickapoo Rangers, had among their company a number of undisciplined rowdies that were in favor of extreme violence and mayhem. Those men were kicked out from the group by Captain Pate and henceforth formed their own band that preyed on travelers south of Lawrence, stealing slaves and reselling them in Missouri.[14] The groups' location was discovered one night after they had been drinking, a company of men then gathered in Lawrence, pursued the renegades, and surrounded them at their camp along the bank of Appanoose Creek in present-day Franklin County.[15] The following account was included in a book published by James Redpath in 1859:

FATE OF THE _____ GUARDS

"But that scene was nothing when compared with the charge on the _____Guards.

Oh, God!"

My friend shuddered violently.

Everybody who is familiar with the history of Kansas has heard of the _____ Guards. They were a gang of Missouri highwaymen and horse-thieves, who organized under the lead of _____ _____ _____, the Kansas correspondent of a leading pro-slavery paper, when the territorial troubles first broke out in the spring of 1855.

After sacking a little Free-State town on the Santa Fe road, and committing other petty robberies and misdemeanors, they were attacked, in the summer of '56, by a celebrated Free-State captain, and defeated by a force of less than one-half their numerical strength. They were kept as prisoners until released by the troops. Capt. _____, satisfied with his laurels, then retired from the tented field. But the company continued to exist and still lived by robbery. Shortly after the Xenophon of the Kansas prairies left them, they elected, as their captain, a ruffian of most infamous character and brutal nature. He presently was known to have committed outrages on the persons of three Free-State mothers.

I will now report the narrative of my friend:

"Capt. _____ and the boys, when they were convinced of the crimes these marauders had committed, resolved to follow them and fight them until the very last man was either banished or exterminated. We heard one night that they were encamped in a ravine near _____. We cleaned our guns, filled our cartridge boxes with ammunition, and left our quarters with as stern a purpose as ever animated men since hostilities were known.

"It was about midnight when we began our march. A cold, misty, disagreeable night. We marched in silence until we came within a mile of the ravine. Then the captain ordered us to halt. There were thirty men of us. He divided us into two companies or platoons in order to get the highwaymen between a cross fire. We could see their camp lights twinkling in the distance. We then made an extended detour and slowly approached the ravine. Not a word was spoken. Every man stepped slowly and cautiously and held in his breath as we drew near to the camp of the enemy. We knelt down until we heard a crackling noise among the brush on the opposing side, which announced the presence and approach of our other platoon.

"The _____ Guards heard it also, and sprang to their feet. They numbered twenty-two men.

"Our captain, then, in a deep, resounding voice, gave the order:

"'*Attention!* Company!'

"The _____ Guards, hitherto huddled together around the fires, tried to form in line and seize their arms.

"But it was too late.

"'*Take aim!*'

"Every man of us took a steady aim at the marauders, whose bodies the camp fires fatally exposed.

"'Fire!'

"Hardly had the terrible word been uttered ere the roar of thirty rifles, simultaneously discharged, was succeeded by the wildest, most unearthly shriek that ever rose from mortals since the earth was peopled.

"I saw two of them leap fearfully into the air. I saw no more. I heard no more. That shriek unmanned me. I reeled backward until I found a tree to lean against. The boys told me afterwards that I had fainted. I was not ashamed of it.

"'March !'

"I obeyed the command mechanically. We marched back in truly solemn silence. I had walked a mile or two before I noticed that the other platoon was not with us.

"I asked where it was.

"*'Burying them,*' was the brief and significant response.

"'Were they all killed, then?'

"'Every one of them.'

"I shuddered then: I can't think of it yet without shuddering."

My friend did not speak figuratively when he said so; for he shuddered in earnest—in evident pain—as he related these facts. But it was not an unmanly weakness that caused it, for he instantly added:

"That scene haunts me. It was a terrible thing to do. But it was right—a grand act of retributive justice—and I thank God, now, that I was 'in at the death' of those marauders. No one ever missed them; they were friendless vagrants. God help them! I hope the stern lesson taught them humanity!

"What do you think of it? Don't you think it was right?"

"It was the grandest American act since Bunker Hill," I said.[16]

Redpath intentionally left the blanks and chose to keep the identity of the massacred group secret, as well as the leader of the free-state group and who his informant had been. This short story may have been forgotten except, in 1900, and only a year before his death, former Danite Richard Hinton came to Topeka to the offices of the State Historical Society, and there he called for a copy of Redpath's book. Upon its delivery, Hinton proceeded to fill in the blanks and identified the massacred group as the Shannon Guards and that the informant, the one that fainted at the scene, was none other than himself. He also named the leader of the Lawrence men as Charles Leonhardt.[17] Of course, we don't know the exact conversation, or whether those assembled understood that there had been two men with almost exactly the same name in Kansas at that time. But as well as Hinton knew Leonhardt, one would think he would have known which one he was talking about.

Did this massacre happen? It remains a mystery. We have seen earlier how Redpath disclosed stories that he was not sure were true concerning Lane and his proposed assassination of Governor Denver, but why would Hinton corroborate the story toward the end of his life and name a man that was obviously his friend as the leader? Those questions remain unanswered. If the massacre happened in the late summer or early fall of 1856, which is the time frame given, then Leonhardt could not have been the leader, as he was still in Plymouth, Massachusetts, operating his gymnasium, according to the advertisments in the paper until January, 1857. This is corroborated by the signing of his citizenship papers on December 3, 1856, and the newspaper story reporting he arrived in early March, 1857.

There is a newspaper transcription from an unidentified paper stating that Leonhardt embraced the massacre story and considered putting it in his book;[18] however, there is no mention of it in any of his writings. And remember, Leonhardt discloses his involvement in the shooting of Van Zumkault, the hanging of a slave catcher, plans to assassinate government officials, and numerous liberating of goods and possessions, so why would he not disclose this if he took part?

One can put together some circumstantial evidence showing the likelihood that, if this massacre happened, then it was Lenhart as the leader. According to G. Brown, Lenhart was a changed man after the Lawrence raid and the *Herald of Freedom* office was destroyed. Lenhart had an earlier connection to the men in the Kickapoo Rangers from his encounter with them after the Battle of BlackJack, and Lenhart was a guerilla captain and had sworn vengeance after the death of young Stewart.

As strange as these coincidences are, Leonhardt's story and entanglement with Lenhart doesn't end there. Just as Leonhardt was a late arriver at the Harper's Ferry scene, so it appears was Charles Lenhart. In an article by Alex Hawes (1881) he described Lenhart as:

> a ne'er-do-well, wild, whiskey-loving fellow. . . . He would get merry as often as—perhaps sometimes a little oftener than—occassion presented itself; but he seemed under all circumstances, to be pervaded by one idea, and that was devotion to Old John Brown and his cause. It was noticed, that if any business of importance was on hand, Charley was always sober, and it was only when all was quiet that he would indulge in his cups. . . . Charles was too dissipated to possess the full confidence of the "Old Cap.," a fact which grieved him much; and when the list was made up for Harper's Ferry his name was not there; for the leader did not know that Charley could control his appetite when necessary. There was no doubt as to his trustworthiness; but the work then in hand demanded not only strong arms and brave hearts, but cool heads. The time of trial came, and singular to relate, on the night before the execution of John Brown, the sentry who stood at the door of his cell, was none other than Charley Lenhart. An hour or two before daybreak, a few hurried words were spoken to the old man—an offer to exchange

clothing and places made. The proffered chance was firmly, sternly refused. Charley implored him to make the attempt to escape, but the answer was:

"It is hopeless—I never should get away, and you would only suffer. No—not a word more, my time has come, and you shall not uselessly sacrifice your life for me." And thus the gallant young devotee, disheartened and disappointed, foiled in his well-planned attempt by the conscientiousness of its object, was next day in the ranks of the militia which stood around the place of execution. . . . The skill with which he planned to get on guard at the cell door on the night before the execution, and the arrangements he made for the escape, attest his faithfulness to his old leader, as well as the reckless daring of his nature.[19]

Unsuccessful in his attempt to free Brown, Lenhart next attempted to free his close friend John E. Cook. Lenhart's obituary relates the following account of this attempt:

When Capt. Cook lay in the famous jail at Charlestown, Va., Charley Lenhart, true to his comrade, made his way there, played proslavery on the "vags;" went to work in one of the printing offices and joined a company then on duty guarding the prisoners. He managed to make himself known to Cook, furnished him the countersigns, arranged a plan of escape, which was to have been carried out one night when Charley was on guard. Cook's anxiety about his sister and brother-in-law, who were then in the town, prevented his making the attempt on the night agreed upon. In the meantime the "chivalry" had one of their spasmodic fits of suspicion, and increased the guard. When the attempt was made it failed, as will be remembered.[20]

That Lenhart had also been in the Danites seems a certainty. We have the note written by General Lane, included in Robinson's (1892) book and G. W. Brown's (1902) book, that mentions Lenhart's planned involvement to take over pro-slavery towns. We have accounts of his alleged involvement with the Reverend Stewart stealing horses in southeast Kansas.[21] And we have the following account in the Lawrence *Republican* of his public threats against Pat Laughlin for Laughlin's part in revealing the secrets of the Danite band in Doniphan County, mentioned in chapter 2. This exchange of letters was given in the Lawrence *Republican* on February 25, 1858:

THE LAST OF PAT LAUGHLIN.—Pat Laughlin, who once made himself notorious by an expose of a secret Free State organization, continued to reside in Doniphan, as the keeper of a grocery or groggery, until a number of boys last week, headed by Charley Lenhart, cleared him out by destroying his liquor and store. Another liquor den was destroyed at the same time. This statement will explain the correspondence subjoined:

LAUGHLIN TO LENHART
Doniphan K T Jan 30 1858.

Mr Lenhart Sir—Reports have come to me, that you openely [sic] expressed in the streets of Doniphan that you were sent from Lawrence K T to kill me, the first opportunity—fearing that the above reports though probably unfounded might lead to a result we might both regret I thought best to inquire of your self if the above reports be tru [sic] and are in fact your intintion [sic]

I am very respectfully   PAT LAUGHLIN
Urbanity of JAMES BUTLER

LENHART TO LAUGHLIN
Doniphan, Kansas. Feb. 1, 1858.

Pat Laughlin: Sir—I have received your letter in which you ask me whether I came here from Lawrence for the purpose and with the avowed intention of killing you.

As I am not in the habit of taking insults, you had better not, in my humble opinion, ask that question more than twice again if you don't want a thrashing. Without urbanity.

CHARLES LENHART.

—Pat left at once, and is now in Missouri—*Crusader of Freedom*.[22]

Lenhart returned to Kansas after his attempted rescues of John Brown and John Cook.[23] During the Civil War, Lenhart joined the Third Regiment under Colonel William A. Phillips and made lieutenant. He died and was buried, according to his obituary, at the camp of the Indian Brigade, somewhere in Arkansas.[24] This obituary or death notice was written for the *Leavenworth Daily Conservative* in May, 1863, and appears to have been written by Richard J. Hinton as "R.J.H." are the intitials printed below the story. This makes more sense when one considers that it was Hinton who later included in his book the story that Lenhart had made connections with the Blue Lodges of Missouri to learn their signs and then used that knowledge to help in the attempted escape of Cook.[25]

11

Conclusion

"The work is finished. American Negro Slavery slain at last. It died very hard."[1] Leonhardt wrote those words in 1876 and they were true; however, he believed his work was unfinished. Leonhardt felt it had become his duty to set down for history the story of the sacrifices of the private soldier during Bleeding Kansas. He knew it would be a race, a race with his own failing health. He wrote in 1878, "Our ranks are getting thinned out. Who knows whose call will be next?"[2] And in a different work, said, "Were it my province to dwell more fully upon what my own experience had been among these working Danites, I would cheerfully make mention of every one of you brother Danites, but this may yet be done if my enfeebled health last a few years longer."[3]

As Leonhardt began his task he remarked:

> It has been a very pleasant duty of mine to mingel [sic] again with some of my former comrades and the promise I then gave you to rescue from oblivion that portion of our Anti-Slavery Struggles in which we had been favored to become joint workers, I hereby, with some misgivings of my ability to do exact justice to all, reluctantly fulfill.[4]

Leonhardt wanted his work to be something more than just about the leaders that people already knew and is illustrated by the proposed titles for his book, two of which were "Stray Leaves belonging to the unwritten history of Kansas humble private men their open works against slavery," and "Stray Leaves belonging to the unwritten history of Kansas privates with the politicians left out."[5] He also noted:

> To the public it must have been very odd to find in Kansas so many military titles among the very first pioneers, who came here to snatch the Virgin Soil from the pollution of slavery. We know all these generals, colonels, majors and captains, even and pass them most willingly over to the next centennial historian to put the wreath of immortality upon their brows! The more he honors them the less apparent becomes the danger of having the private Kansan forgotten.

It would be preposterous of having so large a list of Kansas officers without at least some privates to hold the stirrups even then these private Kansans were wonderful soldiers. Every one of them "acted" when in action as if he had already had his commission of some command in his vest pocket. Still, as they preferred to fullfill [sic] the doctrine that only he is fit to command, who knows how to obey. . . .[6]

Alas, either his failing health or the fact that some parts of his work were destroyed in a fire may explain the reason that he did not fully complete as much of the common history as he wanted to. But what survived, largely unknown for so long, has been well worth the efforts to decipher and untangle in order to gain a better understanding of events in territorial Kansas.

Although he arrived in Kansas in the middle of the struggle, Leonhardt quickly made himself known and became involved with some of the most intriguing and important characters in the unfolding drama that impacted territorial Kansas. His writings provide a rare glimpse into the shadowy and sparsely reported activities of one of the secret groups that was organized to make Kansas a free state. These accounts offer valuable insight into this unknown chapter of Kansas territorial history, as well as a better look at the activity of James Lane, an enigma even to those close to him.

Leonhardt's first-hand accounts of "canvassing" pro-slavery homes before the election on January 4, 1858, including his sketches of conversations, are probably the only ones known in existence and are important to show the workings of common people in the territorial struggle. Today, the modern reader looks back on Jayhawkers as simply one group in the Civil War struggle in Kansas, but, as Leonhardt shows us, there is much more to that story.

One of the main points of his time that Leonhardt disagreed with was the assertion that contemporary writers felt the violence in southeast Kansas had only been a sideshow—that, once peace had been more or less achieved in Douglas and its surrounding counties, the Bleeding Kansas period was over and the territory's admission as a free state assured. In other words, these writers looked down their noses at the fighting in southeast Kansas as petty and insignificant and held the men doing the fighting in contempt as "Jayhawkers." Leonhardt and his compatriots disagreed, however, and felt that if obnoxious pro-slavery settlers had left the northern and northeastern counties only to move into southeast Kansas, then the state was still in danger of becoming slave. Do not forget Leonhardt's use of Montgomery's analogy that these settlers were like ripened weeds and would spread if not cut out.

Along this theme Leonhardt stated his case:

> The future historian may yet take a fearful departure and divide Ks [sic] history in actions had in the counties of Douglas, Shawnee, Jefferson, Leavenworth, Atchison & Doniphan and calling it the Entrance of Slavery into Ks. In those of Johnson, Lykins, (Miami) Linn, Bourbon, franklin, and Anderson—the retreat of Slavery out of Ks. These Border Counties outnumber in local historic places by great odds, those of all the others. Why they have been entirely ignored by those queer bookmakers of ours & their number is great, with a fair prospect of a good crop yet to come, was Never a mistery [sic] to Actors on the borders.[7]

And in a different sketch he noted:

> Bleeding Ks—seems only applicable to Lawrence, or Douglas Co. proper & to Osawatomie & a few other places where the N. England Aid Societies had formed Nuclases [sic] for the rallying of free State men. . . . Troubles on the border have become known as the Jayhawking period where we stole ourself [sic] rich in behalf of Liberty. I challenge them to prove it! There was a good reason for these mistaken ideas—answer. We but never wrote history. Kept the facts to ourselves for prudential reasons & out of pure modesty & laughed heartily at these would be historians who had to write from hearsay only. But the time has Now come in which to lift the curtain a little higher.[8]

Leonhardt spent some time and effort late in his life trying to obtain a government job through some of his earlier connections but was not successful.[9] This seemed to highlight some of the bitterness he had toward the men he felt had profited from what he and others had struggled for. This bitterness is clear, not just that he didn't profit from making Kansas a free state, but that those who did profit ridiculed the very men for the "crimes" they committed in making Kansas free. These "Lookers-on," "Doughfaces," "Fence-sitters," and "Inkslingers,"[10] as he variously called them, were busy writing Kansas history in the 1870s and 1880s and stereotyped the Danites, Jayhawkers, or Niggerthieves as lawless and violent men who only stole from the pro-slavery settlers for profit. Leonhardt not only took exception to this portrayal but turned it on the writers themselves, that they were actually ones who profited from the violence to make Kansas free by writing and publishing accounts, becoming politicians, and participating in land speculation.

The idea that the Jayhawkers or Danites were stealing from pro-slavery settlers and somehow putting the money into a bank account so they would someday be rich was ridiculous, and Leonhardt wanted readers to know they only had to look at those former workers to see the falsehood of this assumption.

The point that the Danites stole from pro-slavery settlers is not in dispute, but Leonhardt obviously felt, as Montgomery had, that in guerilla warfare "the idea . . . is self-sustaining, we . . . say, if you have any money, we must have some of it, and if you have any horses, we must have them for service, etc."[11] This claim is highlighted by Montgomery's statement about returning stolen property after the Denver Peace Treaty. Relating a conversation he had with Judge Wright about indictments for stealing, Montomery wrote, "The judge asked me what the 'boys' would do with their horses. I replied: 'The horses are all the boys have got to show for a year of hard service; they may keep them or sell them, as they please.' . . . He said, *'Tell the boys to do as they damn please with their horses*, they have fairly earned them.'"[12]

Leonhardt even gave us a rule of thumb the Danites used in their stealing—"<u>Horses</u> to use, Oxen to kill I have personal knowledge of. <u>Provisions</u> of all kinds came from proslavery stores but, I never saw <u>furniture</u> taken, as Gov. Sam Medary accuses us of."[13]

To the false accounts of stealing people blind, Leonhardt wanted to say, "Remember not a single one from those actually [sic] working Danites you can point out ever had his prize when the political trader with the money appeared. They still prefer to earn their bread by the sweat of their brow. When the political slate is made up, their names are never on it."[14]

And about those men who helped slaves escape, he said:

UGRR [Underground Railroad] workers Never knew of any other Dividend—than personal toils and untold sacrificing, even unto sufferings of the highest penalties of the Law of that Country, through which perhaps Their Road might open a New feeder into that "historical Great Trunk Road—towards the North Star."[15]

As Goodrich (1998) noted, once Kansas was assured of being free, Montgomery and other radicals continued on as abolitionists.[16] Alluding to this idea, Leonhardt illustrated that, for himself, the lines among Danite, Jayhawker, and abolitionist were, indeed, blurred:

> Among the early free state settlers was a floating populace of young men with fighting proclivities & very restless habits. The moral Element of these Knights of the Spurrs [sic] gravitated into the Abolition ranks & were known as the active working Danites while the remainders by the force of circumstances then prevailing on the one side & the want of all formed equilibrium in their make up only too often made sad mistakes in adjusting cases between <u>thine</u> and <u>mine</u>. Those chaps had Never belonged to the genuine free state party, but were first suffered to act as preliminary surveyors & chain carriers _____ new proposed UGRRoads [sic] and when these feeders to the great trunk road of the north were in running order they worked as Brakemen or firemen on such branchroads [sic] free of cost to us & boarded themselves—Common history gave them the epitath—Jayhawkers![17]

While admitting some excessive stealing went on, Leonhardt contradicted himself somewhat by saying:

> "Jayhawker" was a mere misnomer for Danite. The genuine Danite of the light keepers was never a thief or murderer, neither have I known an assassin among us. That we save from the enemy was but fit and proper Our restless march into Missouri or into the different proslavery settlements on the Border was needed to furnish precedents for Sherman's march to the sea—only it was like the _____ of Columbus, we Danites or Jayhawkers did it first.[18]

Leonhardt was also aware that, although it had been 20 years since the Bleeding Kansas era, it was still too fresh to gain a historical perspective without prejudice, but it was clear he felt there was prejudice against him and other original Danites:

> It is not yet possible to sketch with entire clearness, either a correct and complete history of these events, nor the part even which Brown, Montgomery, Lane and their co-workers have performed. And why is this? you ask; my answer is as follows: Not for lack of unity in action among the different actors in our bloody dramas, but for the continual success among the lookers-on, either to belittle our hard struggle

in the southeastern counties or to make it appear that we only stole ourselves rich in behalf of liberty. Will these illpaid [sic] but over zealous inkslingers [sic] never comprehend the great truth that he who loves liberty, thinks of himself last?[19]

In this passage was one of Leonhardt's passionate points, that those who came later, or never participated in the "real hard work," were the ones writing Kansas history in the 1870s and 1880s and despised those that had done the work. Leonhardt lamented, "Under the Reorganization of the former Lane Danites for political _____, the active Jayhawkers became Known as such and dispised [sic] and outlawed and hated by old friends and foes, for doing the same thing that their brethren [sic] had done north & south of the Kaw River, at the time of 'bleeding Kansas.'"[20]

Leonhardt's answer to those men contained his characteristic humor:

The writer knows many such doughfaces who now a day [sic] pushed themselfs [sic] forward at every town meeting and tells you newcomers to Kansas that he is one of the oldest of early settlers, that he fought at the great battle of Lawrence with John Brown & at the terrible slaughter of Bull Creek with Jim Lane and knows all the early History. While the real fun is all ours! We young & restless men know best, first that these very old settlers never did slept [sic] a single night from home, unless it might have been to jump somebody's claim & got lost in coming home for mother was calling them but second that there never was a fight either at Lawrence not at Bull Creek! And when we young and restless boys from the front now perchance comingle [sic] with some of these old settlers by whom we had perhaps been shamefully critized [sic] in former days, they now overwhelm us with kind words of recognition & hurry to introduce us to Hon. John Doe & _____ Richard Roe as great patriots, statesmen & warriors of bleeding Ks. but always: followers of Brown & Montgomery. Alas, the great Lie swallows entirely the little told truth. sometimes it has happened when thus intorduced [sic] to men of the democratic political _____ south that these same fellow citizen would then step back a few feet, view me all over to make sure how a Danite, Jayhawker, & Niggertheif did look![21]

In the end, Leonhardt remained one of the many hundreds of men who, by taking an active part in the struggle to make Kansas a free state, not only accomplished that goal but also shaped the course of U.S. history, even though their only reward was in satisfaction and not in monetary gain.

Leonhardt was fully aware of the fact that the contest that erupted in Kansas had actually been the opening act that culminated in four bitter years of civil war and the ending of slavery. Toward that end he wrote:

> Most of the Kansas Territorial working Danites have gone to their long homes and mourners go about the streets. What we were as Danites or Jayhawkers, seemed then to all of us of some temporary importance but, that we really were permitted to assist in making not only Kansas a free state but also eventually free our Republic from the curse of Slavery, thus aiding the molding of the future Destiny for millions yet to come, to reap where we sowed, is indeed the only thing of importance left to the few remaining Kansas working Danites.[22]

And in a different document he continued along that theme:

> The Kansas struggles became not only throughout the nation but we saw it shadowing forth in the awakened sentiments of our people who became at last convinced of the dangerous approach the American Republic had made to the brink of a grinding Despotism. We may thus well claim the honor of having here rekindled again the old fire of freedom and confidence in its votaries.[23]

And yet another thought on the connection between Bleeding Kansas and the Civil War:

> As Slavery was a Creature of gross violence and blood, it could only be eradicated by Violence with blood and the clash of Arms!—We have lived to behold the truths of this issue and must become convinced that the Revolution here in Kansas has nobly fulfilled its grand Destiny and that here it was; where Liberty first placed her faithful pickets calling her gallant song to the rescue before her other sons would rush the foe at Appomatix [sic] Courthouse.[24]

In the final conclusion, Leonhardt knew that the satisfaction he and his fellow Danites had gotten from what they had accomplished would be all he received from their work, but he was content with that:

> And now my dear comrades and clever U.G.R.R. fellow experts, let us pause a moment and meditate upon what we went through while working in behalf of the oppressed slave. My own heart tells me, that it was proper and right what little I was favored to do in behalf of free Kansas and for the slave. I have nothing to regret, as even the wish to undo it, but entertain much fear that under equal circumstances I would cheerfully do it over again, only more severely and show no

mercy to the foe of liberty in whatever form or guise he might eventually appear. It is a sad fact indeed, that not one of us active U.G.R.R. private men is well off in these wordly [sic] goods, but who is he that would, if he could bargain away for money consideration his memory in these momentous political events.[25]

And further in a different document he stated:

If it was wicked to help the foot-sore slave along on his road to the north star, or assist other bondsmen directly in the act of stealing themselves, then I must be a very wicked man. . . .[26]

Leonhardt incredulously saw the absurdity in being called a "Niggerthief" for assisting runaway slaves reach freedom, asserting that he and others were only helping those slaves to steal themselves and that the "Manstealers," or slave catchers sent to take runaway slaves back south, were the true "Niggerthieves."[27]

Before he died, Leonhardt was at least aware that a change was underway in the way that other Kansans viewed him and his fellow Danites, and he perceptively noted:

Yes, look up Dear Brothers, especially you, whose gray hairs bespeak your declining years. We will soon have to make room for another generation, who will certainly do honor to our Achievements more fully than most of our fellow men have been permitted to do.[28]

Although Leonhardt wrote that a:

"great change . . . has taken place . . . To be known as a follower of John Brown or James Montgomery brought a temporary stigma to our character, but now the state historical society hunts us up & most flattering regards are send [sic] to us. . . . Even the press of the state becomes warmer in their _____ towards us. No more poisonous ink is slung at us, we are now retired warriors without pay & _____ but still heroes in their eyes,"[29]

he still felt that the doughfaces controlled what was being published as Kansas history.

Perhaps this is the most fitting conclusion I can give Leonhardt today, that Americans in general, and Kansans specifically, gain a better appreciation of the common people in the contest for territorial Kansas and that the struggles in southeast Kansas deserve to be seen with a new appreciation. It is with pleasure that, after 119 years, I have been able to bring Leonhardt's efforts to light.

Epilogue

It seems that in the period following Bleeding Kansas, historians were divided into different camps of who they thought had been the real leader or leaders in making Kansas a free state. People in one camp generally disagreed with people in the other camps, just as James Lane didn't get along with Charles Robinson and George Brown thought very little of John Brown. Although Leonhardt obviously admired John Brown and James Montgomery, and depicted James Lane unfavorably at times as one who was only out for his own political gain, he continued to give Lane credit for his part in making Kansas a free state and at times defended him. But Leonhardt also defended Charles Robinson as well. It is therefore interesting to relate the following analogy that Leonhardt wrote, comparing the different groups of people who were followers of each of the different leaders. He chose to compare each group to different hives of bees.

> The political Aparian [sic] of Kansas can with great exactness show you even now at a glance those distant marks that existed among the genuine early Kansas political bees. We had only three distinct hives. They were known as the Robinson, the Lane and the John Brown bees. The later became afterwards best known as the Montgomery Bees. The Robinson bees were a very noiseless specie and intense workers. Their Honeycombs were all filled even long before the leaves fell from the many political shrubberies that had be[en] send [sic] here from the far Land of the East. The Southern Bear had a peculiar fancy for the New England honey and was openly let loose from the menagery [sic] in LeCompton to rush forth and destroy all Yankee imported colonies. But the strangest thing was these Robinson bees would only buzz around when thus disturbed, but hardly ever stung the Southern Bear to the quick. It was not so with the Lane Bees they had not come out here in a _____ as a swarm of bees does but had found their way to Kansas from every point of the compass and being gathered by the skillful Beeman himself after whom they took the appellasion [sic]. They were original of that stock, which is known as the Common Nation stock, and apt to be improved upon. They did work some Honey they had little inclination to gather. It was a very restless specie. They could sting and they knew that well. Did they meet the Southern Bear, they would crawl all over him and make him howl most terrible. But neither at the battle of Hickory point nor at

Bull Creek did the Beeman Lane become illustrious. On the ____ battle named he was not present ____ fact during the _____ and at the latter he withdrew at sundown delayed operations till early next morning when the southern Bear had cunningly slip [sic] away. The John Brown Bees were the smallest in number, but had no drones among them. When they met the southern Bear they stuck to him till he was finished. They were Never in comfortable quarters. They worked on the Mosaic plan: eye for eye. After these same bees had been gathered into the Montgomery hive, the Honey there began to retreat back into Missouri from where he had strayed. The so-called Montgomery improvement consissted [sic] in the way of providing sufficient needed food to his bees. They were always interrupted in gathering honey and had to be artificially fed, through the guiles from different birds. The beautiful "Jay" and long winged "Hawk" furnished them. By mere jealousy of other Aparians [sic] abroad they became nicknamed the "Kansas Jayhawkers."[1]

Appendix

Ohio City

Checking Leonhardt's statements about Ohio City for accuracy, I found them to be consistent with the little information known about the early town. Writing around 1880, Leonhardt noted that "Ohio City [had] entirely gone out of existennce [sic] and [was] now one of the many farms owned by the Hon. P. P. Elder of Ottawa."[1] Writing about his initiation into the Danites, Leonhardt stated he "arrived at the Hotel of Mr. Wm. Morton at Ohio City."[2] These two statements are supported by Ralph Hobbs' short write-up on the history of Ohio City, where he related:

> The hotel was the first building erected. It was a two-story frame building and the lumber was hauled from Kansas City. A Mr. Morton was the hotel proprietor. This building burned in the year of 1864. The second hotel was built by J. H. Cook. It was used later as a farm home. It was owned and occupied by P. P. Elder. . . .[3]

Further, P. P. Elder's son Aldamer wrote in 1912 about Ohio City that Morton _____ and P. P. Elder bought up the remaining farms for taxes.[4] Both of these statements lend support to what Leonhardt wrote in the 1870s.

Also, in the archives of the Franklin County Historical Society is a letter that corroborates Lane's connection with at least one of the residents in Ohio City. This letter is from C. W. Smith, an undertaker in Lawrence, to George W. Marlin and dated May 20, 1905. In answer to Mr. Marlin's question about Ohio City, Mr. Smith answered, "A note I have enclosed will show you all I know about this site. Abner L. Ross of Ohio came here in Feb—1857—made this city _____. Went south to Neosho River—laid out Ohio City on Middle Creek Franklin Co—with Pete Ridenoure—A R Morton—Wesley Cliff and others—was here at the opening of Eldridge House. Met John Brown—was intimate with James Lane. . . .[5]

Notes

Introduction
1. Leonhardt Collection. Kansas State Historical Society. Manuscript Division.
2. Ibid.

Chapter 1
1. Charles Howard Dickson, " A True History of the Branson Rescue," *Kansas Historical Collections Vol. 13* (1913–1914): p. 296.
2. Charles Robinson, *The Kansas Conflict*. New York: Harper and Brothers, 1892. pp. 51–52.
3. Ibid., p. 160.
4. Thomas Goodrich, *War to the Knife. Bleeding Kansas, 1854–1861*. Mechanicsburg, Pennsylvania: Stackpole Books. p. 49.
5. A. T. Andreas, *History of Kansas*. Chicago, A. T. Andreas, 1883. pp. 99, 425. Leavenworth, Ks. Weekly Herald, May 25, 1855.
6. Dickson, "Branson Rescue," p. 284.
7. Ibid. p. 289.
8. Ibid.
9. Ibid.
10. John H. Gihon, *Geary and Kansas. Governor Geary's Administration in Kansas. With a Complete History of the Territory. Until June 1857. Embracing a Full Account of Its Discovery, Geography, Soil, Rivers, Climate, Products: Its Organization as a Territory, Transactions and Events Under Governor Reeder and Shannon, Political Dissensions, Personal Recountres, Election Frauds and Outrages; With Actors Therin. All Fully Authenticated*. Philadelphia: Chas. C. Rhodes, 1857. pp. 54, 60.
11. G. Douglas Brewerton. *The War in Kansas in 1856. A Rough Trip to the Border, Among New Homes and a Strange People*. New York: Derby & Jackson, 1856. pp. 319–321.
12. George W. Brown, "Reminiscences of Old John Brown," Boyd Stutler Collection. West Virginia State Archives, Vol. 2. 1880. p. 8.
13. Richard J. Hinton, *John Brown and His Men with Some Accounts of the Roads They Traveled to Reach Harper's Ferry*. New York: Funk & Wagnalls Co. 1894. p. 698.
14. D. W. Wilder, *The Annals of Kansas*. Topeka, 1886. p. 91.
15. Leverett W. Spring, *Kansas the Prelude to the War for the Union*. Boston: Houghton, Mifflin and Company. 1885. p. 41.
16. Ibid.

17. William Phillips, *The Conquest of Kansas by Missouri and Her Allies.* Boston: Phillips, Sampson, and Co., 1856. pp. 45–46; Gihon, *Geary in Kansas.* p. 30.
18. Alpheus H. Tannar, "Early Days in Kansas." *Kansas State Historical Quarterly. Vol. XIV. 1915–1918.* p. 226.
19. Charles Leonhardt Collection, Manuscript Division, Kansas State Historical Society.
20. Ibid.
21. Hinton, *John Brown and His Men.* p. 698.
22. Leonhardt Coll.
23. G. Brown, "Reminiscences of John Brown." p. 11, Boyd Stutler Collection.

Chapter 2

1. Bible. Judges. Chapter 13, v. 2–4, King James Version.
2. Ibid. Judges. Chapter 18, v. 1, 2, 9, 11, 16, 18, 20, 27–30, KJV.
3. Harold Schindler, *Orrin Porter Rockwell Man of God Son of Thunder.* Salt Lake City: Univ. of Utah Press. 1966. pp. 24–43, 245, 258–259.
4. Leonhardt Coll.
5. Hinton, *John Brown and His Men.* p. 698.
6. Leonhardt Coll.
7. Letter from Colonel 1444 to Captain 4141, Records of Kansas Territory, Executive Dept. 1854–1861. Territorial Troubles: Danite Lodge, Correspondence and Miscellaneous Records. KSHS Archives Holdings.
8. Frank W. Blackmar, *Kansas A Cyclopedia of State History, Embracing Events, Institutions, Industries, Counties, Cities, Towns, Prominent Persons, Etc.* Chicago: Standard Publishing Co. Vol. 1. 1912. p. 492.
9. Wendall H. Stephenson, *Publications of the Kansas State Historical Society Embracing the Political Career of General James H. Lane.* Vol. III. Topeka: Ks. 1930. p. 92.
10. Records of Kansas Territory, Executive Dept. 1854–1861. KSHS Archives Holdings.
11. For a comparison of the oaths, see John J. Robinson's *Born In Blood The Lost Secrets of Freemasonry.* New York: M. Evans & Co. 1989. pp. 206–207.
12. *Leavenworth Herald.* July 24, 1858.
13. Andreas, *History of Kansas,* pp. 474–475.
14. John N. Holloway, *History of Kansas: From the First Exploration of the Mississippi Valley, to Its Admission into the Union: Embracing a Concise Sketch of Louisiana: American Slavery, and Its Onward March; The Conflict of Free and Slave Labor in the Settlement of Kansas, and the Overthrow of the Latter, with All Other Items of General Interest; Complete, Consecutive and Reliable.* Lafayette, Indiana: James Emmons & Co. 1868. p. 203

15. Ibid.
16. Blackmar, *Cyclopedia of Kansas*, p. 492.
17. Ibid. p. 493.
18. Leonhardt Collection.
19. Ibid.

Chapter 3
1. *Paola Times*. September 18, 1884.
2. Ibid. Leonhardt family papers containing Leonhardt's German military service records.
3. *Pottawatomie Chief*. August 3, 1878; Leonhardt Collection. Last Train.
4. Leonhardt Petition for Citizenship, December 3, 1856. German passport. December 4, 1849. Leonhardt family papers.
5. *Paola Times*. September 18, 1884.
6. Ibid.
7. Ibid.
8. Ibid.
9. Charles Leonhardt Petition for Citizenship. December 3, 1856. Petition No. 349, Circuit Court Common Pleas, Plymouth, Massachsetts. Leonhardt family papers.
10. *Old Colony Memorial*, Plymouth, Massachusetts. June 28, 1856.
11. New England Emigrant Aid Society records. Payments of State Ks. Aid Committee. July 1, 1856 to August 5, 1858. West Virginia State Archives, Boyd B. Stutler Collection.
12. Hinton, *John Brown's Men*. pp. 253–254.
13. *Old Colony Memorial* and *Plymouth Rock*. Advertisements ran on the following dates: May 31, 1856; June 12, 1856; August 5, 6, 7, 1856; and September 13, 1856 through January, 1857. Petition for citizenship, December 3, 1856.
14. *Old Colony Memorial*. June 27, 1857.
15. Emporia, Ks., *Kanza News*. June 6, 1857.
16. Ibid.
17. Joel K. Goodin. "The Topeka Movement." *Kansas Historical Collections*. Vol. XIII, 1913–1914. pp. 238–249.
18. Ibid.
19. *Kanzas News*. June 20, 1857.
20. Ibid.
21. Ibid.
22. Stephenson, *Publications*. pp. 31–32.
23. *Kanzas News*. July 25, 1857.
24. Ibid. August 1, 1857.
25. Ibid. August 8, 1857.
26. *Old Colony Memorial*. September 12, 1857.

27. Samuel Tappan to Thomas W. Higginson, July 6, 1857. Higginson Papers, KSHS, Manuscript Division.
28. Rev. Daniel Foster to Thomas W. Higginson. September 27, 1857. Higginson Papers, KSHS, Manuscript Division.
29. *Kanzas News.* October 3, 1857.
30. Ibid. January 2, 1858.

Chapter 4
1. Leonhardt Coll.
2. Ibid.
3. Andreas, *Kansas*, p. 1066. Holloway, *History of Kansas*, p. 505.
4. G. Murlin Welch. *Border Warfare in Southeastern Kansas 1856–1859.* Pleasanton, Ks: Linn County Publishers, 1977. p. 39; *New York Tribune.* January 8, 1858.
5. Lawrence *Republican*. January 20, 1859.
6. Ibid; Welch, *Border Warfare*. p. 39.
7. T. F. Robley. *History of Bourbon County, Kansas. To the Close of 1865.* Fort Scott, Ks: 1894. p. 83; Welch, *Border Warfare*, p. 39.
8. *New York Tribune.* January 27, 1858.
9. Leonhardt Coll.
10. Clipping from *Leavenworth Daily Times.* October 31, 1870. Hanway Scrapbook, Vol. V. p. 182. KSHS.
11. Leonhardt Coll.
12. Ibid.
13. Ibid.
14. Andreas, *Kansas*. p. 1067; *Herald of Freedom.* March 20, 1858.
15. Harrison Anderson, Letter to Richard J. Hinton. January 27, 1860. Hinton Papers. MSS Division, KSHS.
16. Ibid. *New York Tribune.* February 13, 1858.
17. Martin Litvin, ed., *Prairie Land*, Historical Mother Bickerdyke Collection. Galesburg, Illinois: p. 455
18. Leonhardt Coll. Leonhardt copied this order from papers in James Abbott's possession.
19. Litvin, *Prairie Land*. p. 455.
20. Andreas, *Kansas*. p. 1067.
21. Leonhardt Coll.
22. Stephenson, *Publications*. p. 93.
23. Leonhardt Coll.
24. Ibid.
25. Ibid
26. Ibid.
27. Litvin, *Prairie Land*. p. 455.

28. Leonhardt Coll.
29. Holloway. *History of Kansas*. p. 510.
30. Leonhardt Coll.
31. Ibid.
32. John Speer, *Life of General James Lane, Liberator of Kansas with Corroborative Incidents of Pioneer History*, Garden City, Ks: John Speer Printer, 1896. pp. 167–168; *New York Tribune*. January 27, 1858.
33. Leonhardt Coll.
34. Ibid.
35. Ibid.
36. Ibid.
37. Ibid.
38. Ibid.
39. Ibid.
40. Ibid.
41. Ibid.
42. Ibid.

Chapter 5

1. Leonhardt Coll.
2. Blackmar, *Cyclopedia*. p. 491.
3. Leonhardt Coll.
4. *Pottawatomie Chief*. August 3, 1878.
5. Leonhardt Coll.
6. Ibid.
7. Leonhardt Coll; *Pottawatomie Chief*. August 3, 1878.
8. Leonhardt Coll.
9. Holloway. *History of Kansas*. p. 512.
10. Leonhardt Coll.
11. Welch, *Border Warfare*. p. 64; Holloway, *History of Kansas*. p. 512.
12. Holloway, *History of Kansas*. p. 512.
13. Leonhardt Coll.
14. Ibid.
15. Ibid.
16. Ibid.
17. Ibid.
18. Ibid
19. William P. Tomlinson, *Kansas in Eighteen Fifty-Eight. Being Chiefly a History of the Recent Troubles in the Territory*. New York: H. Drayton, 1859. pp. 191–192.
20. *Herald of Freedom*. January 9, 1858.
21. Leonhardt Collection. *Stray Leaves*.

Notes 115

22. Welch, *Border Warfare*. pp. 61–62.
23. Holloway, *History of Kansas*. p. 512.
24. Leonhardt Coll. Sketchbook
25. Welch, *Border Warfare*. p. 62.
26. Ibid. p. 64.
27. Ibid; Holloway, *History of Kansas*. p. 512.
28. Joseph Williams to Governor Denver. March 5, 1858. Executive Minutes of the Territorial Governors of Kansas, Archives Dept. KSHS.
29. George T. Anderson to Governor Denver. March 27, 1858. Executive Minutes. KSHS.
30. Holloway. *History of Kansas*. pp. 512–513.
31. *Herald of Freedom*. May 8, 1858; Andreas, *Kansas*. p. 1067.
32. Ibid.
33. Andreas, *Kansas*. p. 1068; Welch, *Border Warfare*. p. 69; Letter of Governor Denver to Secretary Lewis Cass, June 23, 1858, in Executive Minutes. p. 533.
34. T. F. Robley, *History of Bourbon County*. p. 86.
35. Lawrence *Republican*. April 29, 1858; Welch, *Border Warfare*, p. 73.
36. Lawrence *Republican*. April 29, 1858; *Herald of Freedom*. May 8, 1858; Andreas, *Kansas*. p. 1068.
37. Lawrence *Republican*. April 29, 1858.
38. Leonhardt Coll.
39. Ibid.
40. Augustus Wattles to William Hutchinson, April 28, 1858. Hutchinson Papers, MSS Division, KSHS.
41. Joseph Williams to Governor Denver. May 18, 1858. Executive Minutes, KSHS.
42. Leonhardt Coll.
43. Tomlinson, *Kansas in Eighteen Fifty-Eight*. p. 135.
44. *Missouri Republican*. May 28, 1858.
45. *Herald of Freedom*. July 19, 1858; Andreas. *Kansas*. p. 1069.
46. Andreas, *Kansas*. p. 1069.
47. *Herald of Freedom*. July 10, 1858.
48. *Pottawatomie Chief*. Aug. 3, 1878.

Chapter 6

1. Leonhardt Coll.
2. George W. Brown. *Reminiscences of Gov. R. J. Walker; with the True Story of the Rescue of Kansas from Slavery*. Rockford, Illinois: G. W. Brown, 1902. pp. 82–90.
3. Ibid. p. 106
4. Ibid. pp. 106–108.

5. Ibid. pp. 108–110.
6. Ibid. pp. 111–112.
7. Leonhardt Coll.
8. *Kansas Weekly Herald.* November, 21, 1857.
9. Stephenson, *Publications*, p. 92. Quotes James Legate in Hinton's *John Brown,* p. 698, Robinson, *The Kansas Conflict,* p. 375, and G. Brown, *Reminiscences of Gov. Walker,* pp. 136–143.
10. Ibid. p. 93.
11. Ibid.
12. *Leavenworth Herald.* May 29, 1858.
13. Leonhardt Coll.
14. Robinson. *Conflict in Kansas.* pp. 378–379.
15. Ibid.
16. G. W. Brown, *Gov. Walker.* pp. 113–114.
17. Ibid. pp. 164–168.
18. Leonhardt Coll.
19. Ibid.
20. G. W. Brown. *Governor Walker.* p. 168.
21. Leonhardt Coll.
22. Ibid.
23. Records of Kansas Territory, Executive Dept. 1854–1861. KSHS Archives Holdings.
24. Blackmar, *Cyclopedia of Kansas,* p. 492; Records of Kansas Territory. KSHS.
25. Records of Kansas Territory.
26. Ibid.
27. Ibid.
28. Brown, *Gov. Walker.* pp. 195–196.
29. Leonhardt Collection.
30. Records of Kansas Territory. KSHS.

Chapter 7

1. Lawrence *Republican.* January 20, 1859.
2. Articles of Agreement for Shubel Morgan's Company in John Brown papers. MSS Division. KSHS; Oswald Garrison Villard. *John Brown 1800–1859: A Biography Fifty Years Later.* New York: Alfred Knopf, 1910. pp. 345, 352–353.
3. Villard, *John Brown.* pp. 354–355.
4. Brown, *Gov. Walker.* pp. 105, 114.
5. Robinson, *Conflict in Kansas.* pp. 360–362.
6. Brown, *Gov. Walker.* p. 114.
7. Leonhardt Coll.

8. Ibid.
9. Ibid.
10. *Pleasanton Observer Enterprise.* March 12, 1925.
11. Leonhardt Coll.
12. Joseph Williams to Governor Denver. March 5, 1858. Executive Minutes, KSHS.
13. Welch, *Border Warfare.* pp. 148–150; Hinton, *John Brown.* p. 191.
14. Lawrence *Republican.* November 11, 1858.
15. Lawrence *Republican.* November 20, 1858.
16. Leonhardt Coll.
17. Ibid.
18. Alpheus Tannar, "Early Days in Kansas," *Kansas State Historical Collections,* Vol. XIV, 1915–1918. p. 226.
19. Leonhardt Coll.
20. Ibid.
21. Villard, *John Brown.* pp. 367–369.
22. Ibid. pp. 372, 379. Villard's account says the slaves were finally placed in the old abandoned preemption cabin on the south fork of the Pottawatomie, south of Osawatomie, and later relates that the cabin was near Garnett; James Hanway and William Ambrose both relate this cabin was near Greeley. James Hanway to F. G. Adams. February, 1878. William Ambrose to F. G. Adams. February, 1878. James Hanway Collection. KSHS.
23. Jessie Carson to H. E. Atchinson. Postmark date is illegible. Author's personal collection.
24. Leonhardt Coll.
25. *Herald of Freedom.* January 22, 1859; Lawrence *Republican.* January 6, 1859.
26. Leonhardt Coll.
27. Villard, *John Brown.* pp. 379–380.
28. Leonhardt Coll.
29. Villard, *John Brown.* pp. 380–381.
30. *Herald of Freedom.* Feb. 19, 1859.
31. Leonhardt Coll.
32. Ibid.

Chapter 8

1. *Kanzas News.* September 25, 1858.
2. *The Lecompton Union.* November 27, 1856; *Leavenworth Journal,* October 29, 1856; Stephenson, *Publications.* pp. 82–83.
3. Stephenson, *Publications,* p. 85, footnote number 7.
4. Hinton, *John Brown.* p. 254.

5. February 15, 1809, Act on Notary Public for the State of Ohio. Mentions no residency requirement. First mention of such is in 1879. Courtesy of Ohio Historical Society.
6. Leonhardt Notary Public Certificate. October 17, 1859. Leonhardt family papers.
7. Hinton, *John Brown*. pp. 254–255.
8. Joe Coppock, "John Brown and His Cause." 1895. p. 325. Boyd Stutler Coll. West Virginia State Archives.
9. B. F. Gue, "John Brown and His Iowa Friends." *The Midland Monthly*. Vol. 7, January 1897. Number 1.
10. Coppock, "John Brown and His Cause." p. 325. Boyd Stutler Collection.
11. Leonhardt Coll.
12. Unidentified newspaper clipping.
13. *Paola Times*. September 18, 1884.
14. Hinton, *John Brown*. p. 254.
15. Ibid. p. 256.
16. Leonhardt Coll.
17. *Pottawatomie Chief*. August 3, 1878.

Chapter 9
1. Leonhardt Coll.
2. *Paola Times*. September 18, 1884.
3. Leonhardt Coll.
4. Ibid.
5. Ibid.
6. Joe Coppock, "John Brown and His Cause." p. 322. Boyd Stutler Collection.
7. Leonhardt Coll.
8. Unidentified clipping of Esther Leonhardt's obituary. April, 1892.
9. Leonhardt marriage certificate. Leonhardt family papers.
10. Field and Staff Muster Roll, 58 Regiment, New York Infantry. Leonhardt family papers.
11. Leonhardt Coll.
12. Field and Staff Muster Roll, 58 Regiment, New York Infantry. Leonhardt family papers.
13. Leonhardt Coll.
14. Unknown newspaper clipping.
15. Charles Leonhardt to Richard Hinton. June 3, 1880. Hinton Collection, MSS Division. KSHS.
16. Thomas M. Carroll, General Affadavit of Caregiver. November 14, 1890. Leonhardt folder. Swan River Museum. Paola, Kansas.

17. Lane *Advance.* July 7, 1882; Partial diary of Charles Leonhardt. June, 1882 to August, 1882. Leonhardt Coll.
18. Lane *Advance.* June 16, 1882. July 7, 1882.
19. Leonhardt Coll.
20. Ibid.
21. Carroll, General Affadavit of Caregiver. November 14, 1890. Leonhardt folder. Swan River Museum.
22. "Cemetery Record A Paola Cemetery," City Hall. Paola, Kansas. 1901. p. 74.
23. F. G. Adams to Esther Leonhardt. April 29, 1885. Leonhardt Coll. KSHS.

Chapter 10
1. Goodin, "The Topeka Movement," *Ks. Hist. Coll.* Vol. XIII. pp. 238–249.
2. *Old Colony Memorial.* April 3, 1858.
3. *Plymouth Rock.* April 8, 1858.
4. Ibid. May 20, 1858.
5. *Herald of Freedom.* April 29, 1858.
6. Leonhardt Coll.
7. G. W. Brown, "Reminiscences of Old John Brown." p. 9. Boyd Stutler Collection.
8. Ibid. p. 4.
9. William Phillips interview with Sheriff Jones. Clipping from *Lawrence Journal.* December 7, 1879. G. Brown, "Reminiscences of Old John Brown," pp. 11–12. Boyd Stutler Collection.
10. *Leavenworth Conservative.* May 2, 1863.
11. Salmon Brown letter to William E. Connelley. November 6, 1913. p. 6; G. Brown, "Reminisces of Old John Brown." p. 75. Boyd Stutler Collection.
12. Robert M. DeWitt, "The Life, Trial and Execution of John Brown." p. 24. Boyd Stutler Collection. West Virginia St. Archives. 1859.
13. Ibid.
14. Ida M. Ferris. "The Sauks and Foxes in Franklin and Osage Counties, Kansas." *Ks. Hist. Coll.* Vol. XI, 1909–1910. p. 350.
15. *Ottawa Herald.* Feb 27, 1988.
16. James Redpath, *The Roving Editor, or Talks with Slaves in the Southern States.* New York: Burdick, 1859. pp. 347–348.
17. Leonhardt Coll. Richard Hinton to Zu Adams, Winter 1900.
18. Unidentified clipping from family papers.
19. Alex G. Hawes, "In Kansas with John Brown." p. 73. Boyd Stutler Collection. 1881.
20. *Leavenworth Conservative.* May 2, 1863; Hinton, *John Brown,* p. 401.

21. Lawrence *Republican*. August 12, 1858.
22. Lawrence *Republican*. February 25, 1858.
23. Villard, *John Brown*. p. 655, footnote 46.
24. Hawes, "In Kansas with John Brown." Boyd Stutler Collection; *Leavenworth Conservative*. May 2, 1863.
25. Hinton, *John Brown*. pp. 396–402.

Chapter 11

1. Leonhardt Coll.
2. *Pottowatomie Chief*. August 3, 1878.
3. Leonhardt Coll.
4. Ibid.
5. Ibid
6. Ibid.
7. Ibid.
8. Ibid
9. D. C. Haskell to Charles Leonhardt, January 31, 1882, March 26, 1882, August 10, 1882; John Martin to Charles Leonhardt, October 23, 1882; George Glick to Charles Leonhardt, December 7, 1883. Leonhardt Collection, KSHS.
10. Leonhardt Coll. *Pottowatomie Chief*. August 3, 1878.
11. Tomlinson, *Kansas in 1858*. p. 135.
12. Lawrence *Republican*. January 20, 1859.
13. Leonhardt Coll.
14. Ibid.
15. Ibid.
16. Goodrich, *War to the Knife*. p. 249.
17. Leonhardt Coll.
18. Ibid.
19. *Pottowatomie Chief*. August 3, 1878.
20. Ibid.
21. Ibid.
22. Ibid.
23. Ibid.
24. Ibid.
25. *Pottowatomie Chief*. August 3, 1878.
26. Leonhardt Coll.
27. Ibid.
28. Ibid.
29. Ibid.

Epilogue
1. Leonhardt Coll. KSHS.

Appendix
1. Leonhardt Coll. KSHS.
2. Ibid.
3. Ralph Hobbs on Ohio City history, October 13, 1960. Hobbs family papers.
4. *The History of Franklin County, Kansas*, Franklin County Historical Society & Friends of the Ottawa Library. Dallas: Curtis Media. 1994. p. S 78.
5. Abner L. Ross to C. W. Smith. May 20, 1905. Franklin County Historical Archives.

Bibliography

Andreas, A. T., *History of Kansas*. Chicago: A. T. Andreas. 1883.

Blackmar, Frank W., ed. *Kansas A Cyclopedia of State History, Embracing Events, Institutions, Industries, Counties, Cities, Towns, Prominent Persons, Etc.* Chicago: Standard Publishing Co. Vol. 1. 1912.

Brewerton, G. Douglas, *The War in Kansas. A Rough Trip to the Border, among New Homes and a Strange People*. New York: Derby & Jackson. 1856.

Brown, George W., *Reminiscences of Gov. R. J. Walker; With the True Story of the Rescue of Kansas from Slavery*. Rockford, Illinois: G. W. Brown. 1902.

Brown, George W., "Reminiscences of Old John Brown." Vol. 2. 1880. Boyd Stutler Collection. West Viriginia Archives.

"Cemetery Record Book A Paola Cemetery." City Hall, Paola, Ks. 1901.

Coppock, Joe, "John Brown and His Cause." Boyd B. Stutler Collection. West Virginia State Archives. 1895.

DeWitt, Robert M., "The Life, Trial and Execution of John Brown." Boyd B. Stutler Collection. West Virginia State Archives. 1859.

Dickson, Charles Howard, "The True History of the Branson Rescue." *Kansas Historical Collections*. Vol. 13. 1913–1914.

Ferris, Ida M., "The Sauks and Foxes in Franklin and Osage Counties, Kansas." *Kansas Historical Collections*, Vol. 11, 1909–1910.

Franklin County Historical Society & Friends of the Ottawa Library, *The History of Franklin County, Kansas*. Dallas: Curtis Media, 1994.

Gihon, John H., *Geary and Kansas. Governor Geary's Administration in Kansas. With A Complete History of the Territory. Until June 1857. Embracing a Full Account of its Discovery, Geography, Soil, Rivers, Climate, Products; Its Organization as a Territory, Transactions and Events under Governor Reeder and Shannon, Political Dissensions, Personal Rencountres, Election Frauds, Battles and Outrages; with Actors Therein. All Fully Authenticated*. Philadelphia: Chas. C. Rhodes, 1857.

Goodin, Joel K., "The Topeka Movement." *Kansas State Historical Collections*. Vol. 13, 1913–1914.

Goodrich, Thomas, *War to the Knife Bleeding Kansas, 1854–1861*. Mechanicsburg, Pennsylvania: Stackpole Books. 1998.

Gue, B. F. "John Brown and His Iowa Friends." *The Midland Monthly*. Vol. 7, January 1897. Number 1.

Hawes, Alex G., "In Kansas with John Brown." *John Brown Pamphlets*, Vol. 4. Boyd Stutler Collection. West Virginia State Archives. 1881.

Hinton, Richard J., *John Brown and His Men with Some Account of the Roads They Traveled to Reach Harper's Ferry*. New York: Funk & Wagnalls Co. 1894.

Holloway, John N., *History of Kansas: From the First Exploration of the Mississippi Valley, to Its Admission into the Union: Embracing a Concise Sketch of Louisiana: American Slavery, and Its Onward March; The Conflict of Free and Slave Labor in the Settlement of Kansas, and the Overthrow of the Latter, with All Other Items of General Interest; Complete, Consecutive and Reliable*. Lafayette, Indiana: James Emmons & Co. 1868.

Litvin, Martin, *Prairie Land*. Historical Mother Bickerdyke Collection. Galesburg, Illinois. 1972.

Phillips, William, *The Conquest of Kansas, by Missouri and Her Allies. A History of the Troubles in Kansas, from the Passage of the Organic Act until the Close of July, 1856*. Boston: Phillips, Sampson and Co., 1856.

Redpath, James, *The Roving Editor, or Talks with Slaves in the Southern States*. New York: Burdick, 1859.

Robinson, Charles, *The Kansas Conflict*. New York: Harper and Brothers. 1892.

Robinson, John J., *Born In Blood The Lost Secrets of Free Masonry*. New York: M. Evans & Co. 1989.

Robley, T. F., *History of Bourbon County, Kansas. To the Close of 1865*. Fort Scott, Kansas. 1894.

Schindler, Harold, *Orrin Porter Rockwell Man of God Son of Thunder*. Salt Lake City: Univ. of Utah Press. 1966.

Speer, John, *Life of General James Lane, Liberator of Kansas with Corroborative Incidents of Pioneer History*. Garden City, Ks: John Speer Printer, 1896.

Spring, Leverett W., *Kansas The Prelude to the War for the Union*. Boston: Houghton, Mifflin and Company. 1885.

Stephenson, Wendall, *Publications of the Kansas State Historical Society Embracing the Political Career of General James H. Lane*. Vol. III. Topeka, Kansas: Kansas State Historical Society. 1930.

Tannar, Alpheus, "Early Days in Kansas." *Kansas Historical Collections*. Vol. XIV. 1915–1918.

Tomlinson, William P., *Kansas in Eighteen Fifty-Eight. Being Chiefly a History of the Recent Troubles in the Territory*. New York: H. Dayton. 1859.

Villard, Oswald Garrison, *John Brown 1800–1859 A Biography Fifty Years Later*. New York: Alfred Knopf. 1910.

Welch, G. Merlin, *Border Warfare in Southeastern Kansas 1856–1859*. Pleasanton, Kansas: Linn County Publishers, 1977.

Wilder, D. W., *The Annals of Kansas*. Topeka, Kansas. 1886.

NEWSPAPERS
Emporia (Kansas) Kanzas News
Lane (Kansas) Advance
Lawrence (Kansas) Herald of Freedom
Lawrence (Kansas) Republican
Leavenworth (Kansas) Daily Conservative
Leavenworth (Kansas) Herald
Leavenworth (Kansas) Journal
Lecompton (Kansas) Union
New York Tribune
Ottawa (Kansas) Herald
Paola (Kansas) Times
Pleasanton (Kansas) Observer Enterprise
Plymouth (Massachusetts) Old Colony Memorial
Plymouth (Massachusetts) Rock
St. Mary's (Kansas) Pottawatomie Chief
White Cloud, Kansas Chief
Unknown newspaper clippings

MANUSCRIPTS
John Brown Papers, KSHS
James Hanway Collection, KSHS
Thomas W. Higginson Collection, KSHS
Richard J. Hinton Collection, KSHS
William Hutchinson Collection, KSHS
Charles F. W. Leonhardt Collection, KSHS

OTHER SOURCES
Feb. 15, 1809 Act on Notary Public for the State of Ohio.
Jesse Carson letter to H. E. Atchinson, circa 1930s, author's personal collection
Hanway Scrapbook, Volume V, KSHS.
Ralph Hobbs' rememberances on Ohio City, Ralph Hobbs Family Papers.
Charles F. W. Leonhardt folder, Swan River Museum, Paola, Ks.
Leonhardt Family Papers
Ohio City Folder, Franklin County, Kansas Historical Archives.
Records of Kansas Territory, Executive Dept. 1854–1861. Territorial Troubles; Danite Lodge Correspondence and Miscellaneous Records. KSHS Archives Holdings.
Boyd B. Stutler Collection, West Virginia State Archives.

Index

A

Abbott, James, 2, 21
Almes, James H., 43
Amnesty Act, 76
Anderson, George
  extract from letter to Governor Denver, 45
  leadership of federal troops, 44
  Paint Creek battle, 47

B

Babb, Edmund, 78, 79
Barber, Robert, 3
Barber, Thomas, 3, 4
Bayne, Oliver P.
  appeal to Lawrence for aid, 44
  photograph, 53
  Squatter's Court host, 20
Bible, Squatter's Court lack of, 22
Big Fan, 32
Black Jack, battle of, 6, 91
Blackmar, Frank, 9, 11
Blue Lodges, 4, 98
Blue Mound, 92
Bondi, August, 23
Branson, Jacob, 2
Brockett, W. B., 46
Brown, George
  account of Lane assassination plans, 63–64
  discussion of fraudulent votes with Gov. Walker, 50–51
  employment of Lenhart, 91
  on John's Brown's Danite connection, 69–70
Brown, John
  account of fleeing settlers, 45
  biographical overview, vii
  defense of Osawatomie, 7
  Lenhart's attempt to free, 96–97
  Leonhardt's comments on leadership, 79–81, 108
  photograph, 54
  possible Danite connections, 69–76
  Pottawatomie Massacre by, 6
  return to Kansas in 1858, 69
Buchanan, Washington, 38

C

Calhoun, John, 64
Campbell, Archie, 43
Candle-box affair, 64–65
Cannons, 44
Carson, Jessie, 74
Carson, Martin, 74
Chase, Salmon P., 77
Clarke, George, 3
Clarke, Malcolm, 1–2
Clark, Jeremiah, 40, 41
Coleman, Frank, 1, 2
Cook, John E.
  disclosure of Harper's Ferry plans, 82
  friendship with Lenhart, 91, 92
  Lenhart's attempt to free, 97
Coppock, Joe, 84
Craig, Jesse, 73
Crowder, T. J., 87
Cruise, David, 74

D

Daniels, Jim, 74
Danites
  breakoff from Lawrence group, 32–33
  covert executions, 42–43

disclosures attributed to Redpath, 10–11, 61
as first offensive free-state group, 37–38
formation of, 8–12, 59–60
Lenhart's membership, 97–98
Leonhardt's initiation, 24–26
Leonhardt's responses to later critics of, 101–6
Mormon group, 8–9, 32
parliamentary procedure, 5–6
questions of John Brown's membership, 69–76
raids on pro-slavery settlers, 33–36
scouting in Missouri, 39–42
secret agents in Missouri, 67–68
secret letters, 65–68
secret oath, 10
Denton, Isaac, 46
Denver (Governor)
  antipathy to Lane, 60
  assassination scheme against, 62
  June 1858 inspection tour, 48
Denver Peace Treaty, 49
DeWitt, Robert, 92
Dorn, Willitz, 43
Dow, Charles, 1, 2
Duke of Desson, 81
Dutch Henry killing, 43
Dutch Henry's Crossing, Pottawatomie Massacre, 6

E

Elder, P. P., 86, 109
Elections
  candle-box affair, 64–65
  January 1858, 37–38
  October 1857 fraud, 1, 50–51
Emporia, Kansas, 16
Ewing, Thomas Jr., 64–65

F

"Farewell to My Comrades," 86
Federal troops, 6, 44, 46–47
Forbes, Hugh, 71, 78
Fort Scott, Kansas, 18
Foster, Daniel, 18
Franklin, Kansas, 7
Free-state legislature, disbanding by federal troops in 1856, 6
Free-state newspapers, destruction of offices, 6, 91

G

Geary City disturbance, 88–91
Gilpatrick (Squatter's Court judge), 21
Goodin, Joel K., 51–52

H

Hamelton, Charles, 48
Hanaway, James, 21
Hanway, John, 87
Hardwick, James, 46
Harper's Ferry raid
  Lenhart's exclusion from, 96–97
  Leonhardt's planned involvement, 79–82
  plans leaked to Secretary of War, 77–78
  result, 78
Hedrick shooting, 46
Herald of Freedom newspaper, 6, 51, 91
Higginson, Thomas W., 18
Hinds, Russell, 76
Hinton, Richard
  allegation that Leonhardt leaked Harper's Ferry raid plan, 77–78
  comment on Leonhardt's arrival in Kansas, 15

comments on Lenhart's attempt
to free Cook, 98
Leonhardt's 1880 letter to, 86
participation in Shannon Guards
massacre, 95
participation in Van Sumbeux
raid, 34, 35
photograph, 55
Hudlow, John, 73
Hungarian Revolt, 13–14

J

Jackson, Jeremiah, 75
Jayhawkers
formation from Danites, 12
Leonhardt's identification of,
103, 104
origin of name, 26, 72
Jenkins, Gaius, 12, 6
John Brown Industrial School
proposal, 87
Jones, Samuel
arrest of Branson, 2
wounding in Lawrence, 6, 91

K

Kaiser, Charles, 43
Kansas Free State newspaper, 6
Kelly, Robert S., 61
Kickapoo, Kansas voting fraud, 50
Kickapoo Rangers, 93
Kilbourn, Henry, 21
Kossuth, Louis, 13, 17
Kuntz, Christ, 42

L

Lane, James H.
accused of involvement in Denver
murder plot, 10
appointed major general by
free-state militia, 24, 60
aspirations to presidency, 30
assassination scheme, 51–52
attempt to control Danites, 12
biographical overview, vii
death threats against pro-slavery
forces, 52–59
first meeting with Leonhardt,
16–17
initiation of Danites at Sugar
Mound, 26
Jenkins shooting, 12, 67
leadership of Franklin raid, 7
Leavenworth Herald criticism,
60–61
Leonhardt's comments on
leadership, 107–8
Leonhardt's growing disenchantment with, 28–31, 70–71
message to Fort Bayne, 23
named to Danite leadership, 3–4, 5
photograph, 56
report on Sugar Mound action,
27–28
rise of influence, 50
secret Danite correspondence,
65–67
Wakarusa War leadership, 3
Laughlin, Patrick, 11, 97–98
Lawrence, Kansas, 1–3, 6–7
Leavenworth Herald newspaper,
10, 60–61
Leavenworth, Kansas, 1–2
Lecompton Constitutional
Convention
free-state threats against,
51–52, 66
Lane's opposition, 59
Legate, James, 5
Lenhart, Charley
acquaintance with Leonhardt, 88
arrival and membership in
free-state forces, 91–93
biographical overview, vii
Danite membership, 97–98
exclusion from Harper's Ferry
raid, 96–97
Geary City disturbance, 88–91

potential involvement in
Shannon Guards massacre, 96
Leonhardt, Charles
account of Denver assassination
plans, 62
account of John Brown's Missouri
raid, 74–75
account of Kuntz killing, 42–43
account of Montgomery's Fort
Scott rescue raid, 73–74
account of Paint Creek battle, 47
account of Squatter's Court, 22
account of Van Sumbeux raid,
33–35
accounts of Lane's assassination
plots, 65
acquaintance with Lenhart, 88
alleged leak about Harper's Ferry
raid, 77–78, 81–82
breakoff from Lawrence Danites,
32–33
Civil War service, 85
comments on candle-box affair, 65
comments on Danite meetings, 6
comments on free-state
leadership, 12, 107–8
comments on mistaken identity
episode, 90–91
comments on Mormon Danites, 9
comments on Republican
convention, 83
criticism of accounts of conflict,
19–20
decision to attend law school, 77
defense of importance of southeast
Kansas struggles, 100–101
early life and service with
territorial legislature, 13–18
growing disenchantment with
Lane, 28–31
head of detachment from
Lawrence, 44
initiation into Danites, 24–26
involvement with John Brown,
70–71, 79–82

marriage, 84–85
photograph, 57
planning of old settlers' reunion,
86–87
preparation of Stray Leaves
manuscript, 85–86, 99–100
questions over involvement
in Shannon Guards massacre,
95–96
rank in militia, 27
recounting of Missouri scouting
party, 39–42
responses to later critics of
Jayhawkers, 101–6
on second order of Danites, 26–27
Underground Railroad trip to
Iowa, 5, 83–84
Leonhardt, Esther
attempts to publish "Stray
Leaves," 87
marriage to Charles, 84–85
photograph, 57
Lewis, Griffith, 82, 84
Little, J. H., 22–23, 73

M

Marais des Cygne Massacre, 48, 75
Marlin, George W., 109
McArthur, L., 62
McCrea, Cole, 1–2
McGee County voting fraud, 50
McLean, L. A., 64–65
Military Board, 63
Missouri raid by Danites, 39–42
Montgomery, James
"attack" on Fort Scott, 43
biographical overview, viii
breakoff from Lawrence Danites,
33
comments on stolen property, 102
cooperation with John Brown,
70–71
destruction of Sugar Mound
ballot box, 42

disbanding of company, 69
discussion with Leonhardt about Lane, 28–29
Leonhardt's comments on leadership, 108
October 1858 attack on, 71
participation in Van Sumbeux raid, 34, 35
photograph, 58
Protective Society leadership, 46–49
rescue raid on Fort Scott, 73
Mormon Danites, 8–9, 32
Morton, William, 109

N

New England Emigrant Aid Society, 15
"Niggerthieves," 106

O

Ohio City, Kansas, 24–25, 109
Old Sacramento, 44
Old settlers' reunion, 86–87
Osawatomie, Kansas, 7, 29–30
Oxford, Kansas voting fraud, 50

P

Paddock, Stephen, 76
Paint Creek, battle of, 47
Paper burghs, 25
Patterson, Billy, 43
Phillips, W. A., 23, 24
Pierson, Thomas, 3
Plumb, P. B., 73
"Plymouth Rock" (gymnasium), 15
Pottawatomie Massacre, 6
Protective Society skirmish with federal troops, 46–47

R

Realf, Richard, 78

Redpath, James
account of Shannon Guards massacre, 93–95
antipathy to Lane, 60–61
photograph, 53
suspected leak of Danite oath, 10–11, 61
Republican Convention of 1860, 83
Rice, Benjamin, 73
Robinson, Charles
capture by pro-slavery forces, 6
criticism of Lane's violence, 62–63
Danite membership, 5, 6
free-state leadership, 1
Leonhardt's comments on leadership, 107
Leonhardt's defense of, 71
Wakarusa War leadership, 3
Ross, Abner L., 109

S

Seaman, Ben, 73
Secret societies, 3–5. See also Danites
Shannon, Wilson, 3
Shannon Guards massacre, 93–96
Slavehunters
Danite retribution against, 36, 76
as true "Niggerthieves," 106
Smith, A. L., 78
Smith, C. W., 109
Snyder, Eli, 75
Southwood-Stone dispute, 20, 22–23
Speer, John, 5
Spurs, battle of, 76
Squatter's Court, 20–25, 87
Stephenson, Wendall, 9
Stevenson, Samuel, 73
Stewart, John E.
accused of plundering and robbing, 46
biographical overview, vii
breakoff from Lawrence Danites, 33

capture by pro-slavery forces, 23
involvement in Kuntz killing, 43
later northern Kansas activities, 84
leadership of Missouri scouting party, 39–40, 41
Leonhardt's Underground Railroad trip with, 83–84
participation in Van Sumbeux raid, 34
photograph, 54
possible raid into Missouri, 75
Squatter's Court service, 21
Stone, William, 20, 22–23
"Stray Leaves," 85–86, 99–100
Sugar Mound conflict, 23–24

T

Tappan, Samuel, 18
Territorial legislature
disbanding by federal troops in 1856, 6
Leonhardt's participation, 16
pro-slavery voting fraud, 1
Thatcher, T. D., 17
Theft
Leonhardt's responses to later accusations, 101, 102, 103
Stewart's forces accused of, 46
Travis shooting, 46

U

Underground Railroad, 5, 83–84, 102

V

Van Sumbeux raid, 33–35, 37
Van Zumkault, 35, 37, 45
Varney, Moses, 78, 82
"A Voice for Kansas," 14–15
Voting fraud
candle-box affair, 64–65
by pro-slavery forces, 1, 50
secret society influence, 4–5

W

Wakarusa War, 3
Walker, Robert J., 50–51, 52
Walker, Sam, 64, 67
Wasson brothers shooting, 46
Wattles, Augustus, 47–48, 51
Wide-Awakes, 5, 20
Williams, S. S., 73
Wood, S. N., 73